dinner is done
simple weeknight recipes from smart in the kitchen

by Marcia Smart

dinner is done
Simple Weeknight Recipes from *Smart in the Kitchen*

© 2022 by Marcia Smart

No part of this book may be reproduced or transmitted in any form or by any means, electronic or mechanical, including photocopying, recording, or by an information storage or retrieval system, without written permission from Marcia Smart except for the inclusion of brief quotations in a review.

Published in the United States by Marcia Smart, SITK Press
smartinthekitchen.com

Library of Congress Cataloging is available upon request.

ISBN: 979-8-9868020-0-8

First Edition

Printed and bound in the United States
Bayside Printing Company, Inc.

Book Design: Elise DeSilva, Limb Design
Book Editor and Production Manager: Roni Atnipp
Photography: Debora Smail
Food Styling: Marcia Smart

In the making of this book, every attempt has been made to verify names and facts. We apologize if any errors have been made.

Dedication

For my parents, who always made family dinner a priority and to this day think everything I make is the best thing they've ever tasted. And for my three children and my husband who inspire me in countless ways. Here's to a million more family dinners. I love you!

Table of Contents

6 — Foreword

8 — Good Ingredients

14 — Smart in the Kitchen School

16 — Family Dinners

20 — Salads

42 — Meatless Mains

74 — Fish

96 — Meaty Mains

122 — Soups + Stews

142 — Sides

168 — Snacks

188 — Dessert-*ish*

212 — Cocktails

230 — Kitchen Equipment 101

232 — Acknowledgments

234 — Index

240 — About Marcia

> I don't call myself a chef. That's an industry term reserved for those who run restaurant kitchens. But I can help a busy mom get dinner on the table as if her life depends on it.

When I look back on this incredibly lucky life as a food writer, recipe developer and culinary instructor, I almost feel shocked at how fortunate I've been, and I can't quite put my gratitude into words. It's funny where life takes you. If someone had suggested to me when I was 25 that I'd spend almost three decades as a cooking instructor, I might have looked very confused. Sure, I wanted to work as a writer for *Food & Wine* or *Travel + Leisure*, but instead I started out as a fact-checker at *Parenting* magazine in the New York editorial office. But eventually, the low pay of magazine journalism in Manhattan led me to return to my native California, where I would meet and fall in love with my husband. A mutual passion for travel, restaurants, cooking and wine is what started our "when you know, you know" romance. And soon, a severance check from my dot-com stint as a website producer allowed me to enroll in culinary school—and as they say, the rest is history.

During my culinary training, I always volunteered to assist visiting chefs and help with private evening events. Just after I finished cooking school, co-teaching a six-week basics course inspired a true joy for teaching. That moment when someone feels confident in the kitchen, when they realize they can do it, it lights me up. Fast forward, and a move to Houston, Texas, had me arranging cooking classes so I could meet other moms and maybe make a few friends. Those mom friends would tend to ask what I was making my kids for dinner, as if because I wrote for *Cooking Light* it must be something magazine worthy. But no, it never was. It was always simple, pared-down food that satisfied but also checked a box: It got dinner on the table with the least effort possible, so there was still some energy left to bathe and read to three kids under five years of age. Dinner was more of a strategy than a passion play, and there were tricks up my sleeve from years as a food writer and instructor. In my role as the founder of *Smart in the Kitchen*, it's been my mission to share and teach those tricks to my students and community.

Where I'm sitting now, with one child embarking on college and two more in high school, I can't believe I'll have only four more years of family dinners as I know them. I'm sure we will still get together as our core family of five for holidays and summer travel. But those times won't be my day-to-day anymore. What once felt like an endless rotation of dinners and cleanup and homework now feels like life's greatest and most fleeting gift.

So this, my friends, is my gift to you in return. I want to simplify your dinner routine while keeping it delicious. I want to gift you time and energy for your family. I want you to soak up the people you love most. Because before you know it, your table might look different. I hope these recipes help you in some way, and I hope your dinners spark more joy and laughter and less stress. I want you to look at the photos on these pages and say, "I can do that!" You, and the people at my own table, are the reason I do what I do.

xo,
Marcia

Good Ingredients Make a Difference

It's true: If you use cold-pressed extra virgin olive oil instead of subpar and super processed olive oil, it's going to make a difference. Use good salt. Use fresh herbs and citrus. Seasonal produce always tastes better, the more local the better. Shop at a farmers market or subscribe to a CSA (Community Supported Agriculture) or farm delivery to help you eat in season. I like nothing better than a Saturday stroll through my local farmers market with a coffee in hand. Maybe even from your own backyard. Use good-quality meat, from local producers if possible, and the best way to source that is usually at your local farmers market. While I think flash-frozen fish can be a great buy, you don't want to purchase shrink-wrapped meat that's been sitting around for who knows how long. I'll never forget the time I picked up a package of grass-fed ground beef and turned it over to realize it was imported from Australia. Australia! Not a local buy for me. When in doubt about how and what to eat, follow writer and journalist Michael Pollan's mantra. "Eat food. Not too much. Mostly plants." And while I love meat, I try to balance it with lots of vegetables! Another good rule of thumb: Don't eat anything your great-grandmother wouldn't recognize as food.

Salt + Pepper

Salt is probably the ingredient that can make the biggest impact on your cooking. Salting well is an art form that will enhance the flavor of food and create a finished dish that tastes more inherently like what it is, not just salty. Ditch the generic iodized table salt, which tastes metallic and sharp, and opt for flaky kosher salt. Many chefs and culinary professionals prefer Diamond Crystal kosher salt, which is flaky and light and has more volume and surface area than grains of table salt. I always like to finish what I'm cooking with a sprinkle of a coarse salt, like fleur de sel or Maldon sea salt, and use coarse salt as topping for chocolate chip cookies or brownies. It creates that salty-sweet-crunchy trifecta.

I use only freshly ground pepper from a pepper mill, which is coarse and flavorful. Fill your grinder with either a colorful peppercorn blend or black peppercorns, whichever you prefer. Pre-ground pepper in a spice container tends to be powdery and the flavor can be overpowering. You could also use a mortar and pestle to grind peppercorns to your desired texture. Ground pepper can be tricky to measure and the amount in a recipe is a personal preference. The measurements called for in this book are a suggestion, so add as much or as little as you'd like.

Cooking Oils

Extra virgin olive oil and avocado oil are what I use most often. Avocado oil can be used instead of vegetable or canola oil in any recipe, including boxed brownie or cake mixes. It's flavorless and can be used at high heat. Look for 100 percent unrefined extra virgin olive oil that's cold pressed with a harvest date; bonus points if it's organic. Olive oil shouldn't be aged like wine; use it up as soon as you buy it. When I'm cooking in a vacation rental or someone else's home, I always smell the olive oil before using it. It should smell like olives, not rancid, acidic or sharp. I also use toasted sesame oil for flavoring Asian-inspired dishes.

Soy Sauce, Tamari and Coconut Aminos

Buy organic soy sauce whenever possible. In general I prefer a low-sodium version. Tamari has a deeper, more reduced and richer flavor. Coconut aminos have a fermented flavor like soy sauce, but they're made with coconut so they're soy free. My favorite option of the three is gluten-free organic tamari.

Fresh Squeezed Juice

Fresh citrus has such a superior flavor to bottled varieties. When I call for lemon, lime or orange juice in a recipe, I always mean freshly squeezed. I use a handheld citrus press that keeps the seeds out of the juice. If you're using zest in a recipe, be sure to zest before juicing. Cut citrus crosswise through the middle to juice it; place the cut side facing down in a citrus press to extract the most juice. For wedges, cut lengthwise through the stem end. If you cut slightly off center, you'll miss the seeds that run down the middle.

Organics

It's not necessary to purchase *all* organic produce. Consult the "Dirty Dozen" list from the Environmental Working Group at ewg.org for the vegetables you may want to buy organic.

Stock vs. Broth

These two liquids are basically made from the same ingredients and home cooks often use the terms interchangeably. However, stock is used as a base for soups, stews and sauces and broth is more flavorful and can be sipped on its own. The fundamental difference is that stock is unsalted and is made from water and bones (sometimes roasted, sometimes not) along with aromatics like onion, carrot and celery (mire poix). Broth can be cooked with meat or vegetables and is often seasoned. Stock tends to get a thicker consistency from the bones and cartilage that break down in the liquid as it cooks. Broth is sometimes made with strained stock as well as flavorings, such as fresh herbs, pepper and salt. It can then be sipped on its own. "Bone broth" has become trendy in recent years. It's a term for any stock or broth simmered with bones long enough for the collagen to break down and add a gelatinous quality to the finished product. In cooking school, we would make what was called a "double stock," which is just using stock as the base for simmering roasted meat bones and more aromatics—it's a delicious and flavorful base for any soup or sauce. Anything labeled as vegetable stock or vegetable broth is the same, since neither contains meat bones, although vegetable broth may have more salt added.

Carrots

There's no need to peel carrots when cooking at home; just wash them well. (My French cooking school instructors would not approve if they knew I wasn't telling you to peel and square off carrots before chopping them!) Scrub them under running water, similar to how you'd wash a potato that you're leaving the skin on.

Cheese

Parmigiano-Reggiano is made in a designated region in Italy and aged at least one year. Often, Americans use the generic term "parmesan" to refer to Parmigiano-Reggiano. In the recipe ingredient lists here, we always use freshly grated Parmigiano-Reggiano. When purchasing, look for the Parmigiano-Reggiano stamp on the rind. You can purchase it in large wedges and grind it yourself in a food processor or grate it on a Microplane as needed. Be sure to save the rinds to use in soups and tomato sauces.

I generally shy away from all packaged pre-grated cheeses because of the cellulose that gets added to the package. It can make cheese taste chalky and creates a dry texture. Look for sheep's milk feta from Israel, Greece or France stored in brine, instead of pre-crumbled. Feta packed in brine is creamier and doesn't contain the potato starch or cellulose powder usually found in pre-crumbled cheeses.

Garlic

In the grocery store, I look for garlic with a dirty root end. That may sound strange, but a little dirt at the root base shows that the garlic hasn't been bleached, which can be the case for garlic imported in huge tankers from other countries. The best bet is to purchase garlic from a farmers market.

To cut garlic, cut off both ends of each clove to release the skin. Now the clove can be smashed and peeled, then chopped or minced. You can also grate a whole garlic clove on a Microplane to create a fine paste.

Fresh Herbs vs. Dried

Whenever possible I prefer the flavor of fresh herbs. They're easy to grow in pots at home; I have pots of rosemary, mint, chives, parsley, oregano and thyme growing year-round. Basil gets planted in spring or in the early summer and grows like crazy all summer long. Generally, you can substitute a tablespoon of fresh herbs for a teaspoon of dried.

Organizing Spices

I organize my spices the same way my cooking school did. Sweet spices are together on one shelf: cinnamon, ginger, allspice, nutmeg, cloves, etc. Savory spices are on another shelf: cumin, paprika, onion and garlic powders, chili powder, crushed red pepper flakes. Specialized international spices are together on another shelf: garam masala and Korean chile flakes, along with anything I don't use regularly.

Don't throw spices away just because their expiration date has passed. Smell them to gauge whether they're still good. Do they smell like what they are? Or have they lost their aroma? Depending on the answer to that, keep or toss.

Smart in the Kitchen School

I launched my blog, **smartinthekitchen.com**, almost a decade ago as a way to share my family's weekly meal plan and the hundreds of recipes I've developed over the years. During the pandemic, I created a second site, **smartinthekitchenschool.com**, where I host a cooking school membership and share teaching videos and online classes.

Smart in the Kitchen School became a way for me to continue teaching cooking classes virtually while still connecting with my students. Along with the monthly school membership, *Smart Knife Skills* is an online course for home cooks with recorded lessons and recipes to help you practice (and speed up) your prep skills. For those who want to master meal planning, I've created a five-part recorded meal planning course that will get your weeknight dinner routine down to a science.

How to Write a Shopping List

I use a handwritten shopping list organized into a grid that's based on the layout of the store. I draw a cross on a sheet of paper to divide it into four sections. The top left section is produce because that's the first area in the grocery store. The top right section is meat and seafood. Bottom left is dairy and deli. Bottom right is dry goods from the aisles in the middle of the store and frozen items.

How to Time a Recipe

Underline anything that needs to be prepped. Write a time estimate in the margin for how long it will take you to prep each item. Underline cooking time cues. Add it all up to get an idea of the total time it will take to make that recipe. That will be different for everyone. It may take a trained chef 15 minutes to prep everything, but a home cook an hour. Make an estimate of how long it will take you. Once you get in the habit of reading recipes this way, you'll have an accurate idea of how long recipes will take you to prep and cook. You will also be able to time multiple recipes to finish cooking at the same time.

Mise en Place

Everything in its place. Read the recipe from start to finish. Get out all the ingredients. Slice, cut, chop. Now you can begin cooking.

Taste as You Go

This might be the most important lesson here. Taste as you go, adjust and refine. You'll become an intuitive cook who can tweak a dish to your liking.

Last But Not Least

Don't stress! Substitutions are okay and listed for many of the recipes in this book—make it work for your family and the flavors they prefer.

Thoughts on Family Dinner

It shouldn't be about rules—it should be about sitting down with the people you love and enjoying a good meal. But there are some basic guidelines for family dinner that frame a positive experience at the table and teach good manners and open communication. Face-to-face communication is a dying art in today's culture. We are often hunched over the glow of electronics, communicating through DM, tweets, texts or emails. I've been guilty of texting my own kids to tell them dinner is ready when we're all in the same house. Please don't judge me; my only excuse is that I can't stand yelling.

Sitting down to family dinner is the ultimate intro lesson in social graces. And it's becoming rare in a way that makes it feel old-fashioned and semi-obsolete. Dinnertime can teach children (and their parents) how to share information in real time, take turns listening and talking, pace a conversation and ask questions. A conversation is an art form. In my humble opinion, teaching our children how to converse one on one may be more crucial than their learning math facts. But maybe that's just because for me, math is hard and talking is easy. That's not to say that it's wrong in any way to make a plate and head into the family room to watch a football game or Friday night movie.

There are so many statistics about the benefits of family dinners. Family dinner is good for our children's vocabulary and our teenagers' mental health. It should also be a safe space, not the place for lectures. The actual cooking of dinner shouldn't be so complicated that it stresses us out and kills the joy of sitting down and sharing a meal with the people we love. While children are young and have early bedtimes, a parent may need to sit down to feed them before they're ready to eat dinner themselves. There are also nights when school-age kids have late games or sports practices, or someone in the family is eating at an earlier or later time—as long as someone sits down to talk with and keep that child company, it still counts as a family meal in my book. And if dinnertime becomes a stressor, use other opportunities for quality time. Walk together around the neighborhood or play Rummikub or Uno without phones present. You've got this!

> The actual cooking of dinner shouldn't be so complicated that it stresses us out and kills the joy of sitting down and sharing a meal with the people we love. //

Rules for Family Dinner

Feel free to adopt these or create your own. Just start creating a dinner routine, and make it a priority. While we definitely have our fair share of dinners when someone ends up in tears, one sibling is mad at another, or things don't go as planned, this has helped me over the years create a habit to sit down together.

1) No phones or electronic devices of any kind. TV off. Music encouraged.

2) Set the table. We use inexpensive placemats and paper napkins. Nothing fancy—it's more about the ritual. But you can use cloth napkins that are machine washable and inexpensive. Or mix and match vintage plates. Let your kids set the table when possible. Sometimes I just set out all the components for the table and let everyone help set up their spot as they make their way into the kitchen.

3) Napkins in laps.

4) Take turns to talk and listen. It can be difficult for all of us, but it's a learned skill. Practice starts at home.

5) This is not the time to harp on less-than-stellar grades, behavior, messy rooms or athletic performance. Think of your dinner table like Switzerland: a neutral territory. There's a time for all of that later.

6) Share a rose and a thorn: a nugget of something exciting or positive that happened during the day and anything that was tricky or challenging. It's a great conversation starter. My youngest created "leaves" that are just stories that aren't really good or bad; they're just eminently shareable.

7) Laugh.

8) Chew with your mouth closed.

9) Clear your dishes. Rinse them. Actually put them inside the dishwasher.

10) Be thankful, grateful and polite to the cook. Someone planned, shopped for, prepped and cooked the dinner (most likely you!). A simple "thank you" will suffice. Even if someone else doesn't particularly like what's for dinner, they don't need to announce it. If they've honestly tried at least a couple of bites and still don't like it, they're welcome to make themselves a sandwich. But nothing that requires pots and pans, because no one needs more dishes to wash!

Salads

A general rule for salads: Whatever your family will eat is the name of the game.

I prefer simple and seasonal salads, especially on weeknights when time is at a premium. I want the healthy addition of fresh greens with a simple, tangy salad dressing—and I have just the one at the end of this chapter!

A big green salad with my Super Simple Salad Dressing (page 40) is my go-to about 90 percent of the time. I typically don't give exact amounts of dressing to add to my salad recipes because, in my opinion, it's a personal preference. Just don't drench your leaves so much that there's dressing pooling at the bottom of your salad bowl! You can always add more, but you can't "undress" a salad. You could, however, add more lettuce to soak up extra dressing in a pinch.

If you're looking for a colorful winter salad, try the Collard Greens and Brussels Sprout Salad (page 26). I promise fresh collard greens are mild and delicious. Serve it for Thanksgiving as the perfect no-wilt salad. My favorite from this chapter is probably the Kale Caesar (page 28), with a shortcut dressing that's fast enough for a weeknight.

One tip for kids: Set up a mini salad bar. Kids are more likely to try new things if they're in charge. The salad bar doesn't need to be elaborate. Besides salad greens and dressings, add small bowls of cherry tomatoes, sliced or shredded carrots, cucumbers, avocados, bell peppers or grated cheese. Works every time!

24
Butter Lettuce, Radish and Radicchio Salad

26
Collard Greens and Brussels Sprout Salad

28
Kale Caesar

30
Corn, Zucchini and Tomato Salad

32
Red Cabbage Slaw

34
Salmon Salad "Niçoise"

36
Quick-Pickled Red Onions

38
Homemade Buttermilk Ranch Dressing

40
Super Simple Salad Dressing

 **SMART tip** Don't forget to salt your salads! After you add the dressing, toss with kosher salt. It will stick to the leaves and enhance the flavor. I like to finish my salads with one last sprinkle of coarse salt, which adds a delicious salty crunch.

Butter Lettuce, Radish and Radicchio Salad

Serves 4 to 6

1 head radicchio, halved

2 heads butter lettuce, roughly torn

2 or 3 green onions (white and green parts), thinly sliced

3 breakfast radishes or 1 watermelon radish, trimmed and thinly sliced

1 tablespoon chopped fresh chives

1 tablespoon chopped fresh mint leaves

Super Simple Salad Dressing (page 40)

¼ teaspoon kosher salt

Garnish (optional): Additional chives or mint leaves

Cut the radicchio in half lengthwise (through the root end) and cut out the white triangular core at the base. Place half the radicchio cut side down on a cutting board and slice crosswise, starting from the top and shaving it as thin as possible; reserve the second half for another salad. Add the radicchio to a salad bowl along with the lettuce, green onions, radishes and herbs.

Toss with the dressing, enough to just coat the leaves without any pooling in the bottom of the bowl. Sprinkle with the kosher salt and taste for seasoning; adjust if necessary. Add torn fresh herbs if you like.

 **notes**

If you don't like the bitter flavor of radicchio, use extra baby gems, red leaf lettuce or romaine hearts.

SMART tip: The beauty of this salad is that it can be tossed 30 to 45 minutes before serving because the collard greens and Brussels sprouts don't wilt.

Collard Greens and Brussels Sprout Salad

Serves 6 to 8

1 bunch collard greens (about 8 leaves)

1 pound Brussels sprouts, roots trimmed, shredded in a food processor

4 ounces pecorino or Parmigiano-Reggiano cheese, freshly grated on a Microplane (about 1 cup)

1 large Honeycrisp apple, cut into ½-inch dice (no need to peel)

½ cup pecan pieces

Super Simple Salad Dressing (page 40)

1 cup pomegranate seeds

Coarse salt, to finish

Cut out the center stem of each collard leaf. Stack the leaves and cut crosswise into thin strips, then chop the strips into bite-sized pieces. Transfer to a salad bowl.

Add the Brussels sprouts, cheese, apple and pecans. Add the dressing, enough to coat the leaves without any pooling in the bottom of the bowl. Toss to combine and sprinkle with the pomegranate seeds and coarse salt.

notes

There's no need to peel the apple; the skin adds color and texture. If you don't have a food processor, thinly slice the Brussels sprouts by hand. You can also buy bagged presliced Brussels sprouts to save time. You might have the wrong impression of raw collard greens, so please try this with collards at least once! But if you must, feel free to use kale or spinach. If you can't find pomegranate seeds, add a cup of halved red seedless grapes or dried cranberries.

SMART tip: If the bowl spins while you whisk in the olive oil, place it on a kitchen towel or damp paper towel to keep it stable. Don't use store-bought bagged kale because they don't remove the center stem.

Kale Caesar

Serves 4 to 6

1 teaspoon anchovy paste or 1 anchovy fillet, finely chopped

1 garlic clove, grated on a Microplane or minced

2 tablespoons fresh lemon juice

2 tablespoons Dijon mustard

2 tablespoons good-quality mayonnaise

¼ teaspoon kosher salt

⅓ cup extra virgin olive oil

20 large stalks curly or lacinato kale, center stems removed, roughly torn

Garnish (optional): Shaved Parmigiano-Reggiano cheese; thinly sliced radishes; Quick-Pickled Red Onions (page 36); Spicy Roasted Garbanzos (page 183)

In a wooden salad bowl, mix the anchovy paste, garlic and lemon juice. If you have time, let this sit for 10 minutes or so to mellow and combine the flavors. Whisk in the Dijon mustard, mayonnaise and salt until combined. Slowly drizzle in the olive oil while whisking to emulsify. Pour out about half of the dressing into a small bowl.

Add the kale to the salad bowl and toss to combine. Top with a drizzle of the reserved dressing and toss again. Taste a leaf to make sure the salad is well dressed. Finish with your choice of garnish. If you're left with extra dressing, cover it and store in the refrigerator for up to a week.

This salad is delicious topped with rotisserie or grilled chicken, flank steak or roasted salmon.

notes

I've used the same wooden salad bowl for over 20 years. Making dressing in the bowl keeps it from drying out over time. I never soak it in water, which would have ruined and cracked it. If you don't have a wooden salad bowl, any large salad bowl will work. Lacinato kale may be labeled as Tuscan or "dinosaur" kale. You can also use curly red or green kale, but be sure to remove the center stems, which are woody and tough. Someone in the family hates kale? Use romaine lettuce instead.

SMART tip: When cutting corn kernels off the cob, stand the ear up in a large bowl and use a chef's knife to slice off the kernels so they fall into the bowl. Don't stand it directly on a cutting board or they will roll all over the board and kitchen counter!

Corn, Zucchini and Tomato Salad

Serves 6

- 4 tablespoons extra virgin olive oil, divided
- 3 cups fresh corn kernels cut off the cob (about 4 large ears)
- ½ teaspoon kosher salt
- 1 zucchini, trimmed and diced (no need to peel)
- ½ cup halved red or yellow cherry tomatoes
- 2 ounces feta, finely crumbled, or grated Cotija cheese (about ½ cup)
- 4 green onions (white and green parts), sliced
- ½ cup packed fresh cilantro leaves, chopped
- 1 jalapeño chile, seeded and finely chopped
- 1 or 2 garlic cloves, finely grated on a Microplane or minced (1 to 2 teaspoons)
- Finely grated zest of 1 lime (optional)
- 2 tablespoons fresh lime juice
- Chili powder or crushed red pepper flakes
- Coarse salt and freshly ground black pepper, to finish
- 1 avocado, pitted, peeled and diced (optional)

In a large skillet or wok over high heat, warm 1 tablespooon oil. Add the corn and salt, and cook about 2 minutes. Add the zucchini, stir, and cook until the corn and zucchini are softened, 3 to 4 minutes. Set aside to cool to room temperature.

In a large mixing bowl, add the corn, zucchini, tomatoes, cheese, green onions, cilantro, jalapeño, garlic, lime zest if using, lime juice, the remaining 3 tablespoons olive oil and chili powder to taste. Gently toss to combine. Taste and adjust seasoning with salt and pepper, lime juice or chili powder. If you like, top with the avocado. Serve immediately.

This salad makes a delicious side to roasted salmon, grilled chicken or flank steak. Or scoop the corn salad into halved avocados as a serving vessel. This is also good served over salad greens.

notes

This is best with fresh summer corn, but it's fine to substitute frozen. Use parsley if you're not a cilantro fan. You can use yellow summer squash instead of zucchini, or add a diced red or yellow bell pepper for color. Just remember, if you add more veggies, you may need more lime juice and olive oil to bring the flavors together.

 **SMART tip** This slaw is really best when it sits for at least 30 minutes at room temperature before serving. You can make it earlier in the day; just cover and refrigerate. Let it come to room temperature and taste again before serving; add more dressing and salt if needed.

Red Cabbage Slaw

Serves 4 to 6

3 tablespoons red wine vinegar
3 tablespoons apple cider vinegar
½ teaspoon garlic powder
¾ teaspoon kosher salt
½ cup avocado oil
1 medium head red cabbage, about 2 pounds
2 tablespoons minced fresh chives
2 tablespoons minced fresh dill
2 tablespoons minced fresh flat-leaf parsley
Freshly ground black pepper
Coarse salt, to finish

In a salad bowl, whisk together the red wine vinegar, apple cider vinegar, garlic powder and kosher salt. Whisk in the oil to emulsify. Transfer about half of the dressing to a small bowl to make sure the slaw doesn't get overdressed.

Slice the cabbage in half through the root end and cut out the white triangular core at the base. Place the cabbage cut side down and slice it crosswise, starting from the top, as thin as possible. Add the cabbage, chives, dill, parsley and pepper to the bowl and toss to combine with the dressing. Taste to make sure the slaw is well dressed, adding more dressing if necessary. Finish with a sprinkle of coarse salt.

Serve as a side salad to grilled meats or Dry-Rubbed Pulled Pork sliders (page 106).

notes

Add more fresh herbs if you prefer. You can also add 1 to 2 grated carrots for color, but as they sit with the cabbage they will turn slightly red!

SMART tip: This is delicious for using leftover cooked salmon from Sockeye Salmon with Haricots Verts and Cherry Tomatoes (page 88). If you don't have leftover cooked salmon, use canned wild salmon. Or you can make this as a tuna salad niçoise instead.

Salmon Salad "Niçoise"

Serves 4

- 1 pound cooked salmon, skinned if necessary and flaked (2 to 3 cups)
- ¼ cup minced shallot or red onion
- ½ cup diced celery (about 2 stalks)
- ¼ cup chopped cornichons or dill pickles
- ¼ cup minced fresh flat-leaf parsley
- ½ teaspoon hot sauce (such as Tabasco or Crystal)
- 1 teaspoon Old Bay Seasoning
- ½ cup good-quality mayonnaise
- 2 teaspoons Dijon mustard
- ½ teaspoon kosher salt
- Freshly ground black pepper

To assemble the "Niçoise" Salad
- 2 heads butter lettuce
- 1 cup cherry tomatoes, halved
- 8 ounces green beans, blanched and cooled
- 2 to 4 hard-boiled eggs, peeled and quartered
- 4 small Yukon gold potatoes, cooked and quartered (no need to peel)
- Super Simple Salad Dressing (page 40)

Additional toppings (optional): Diced avocado; Quick-Pickled Red Onions (page 36); chopped green onions or fresh herbs

In a medium mixing bowl, use a fork to mix together the salmon salad ingredients. Taste and adjust the seasoning if necessary. Set aside.

To assemble the niçoise salad, layer lettuce leaves on four individual plates. Top each with a scoop of salmon salad. Around the salmon salad, arrange the cherry tomatoes, green beans, hard-boiled eggs, potatoes and additional toppings of choice. Drizzle with dressing to taste.

notes

Small French cornichons and dill pickles add a briny, tart flavor to the salmon salad. I prefer to chop them by hand instead of using dill pickle relish because of the crunch and texture they add.

 **SMART tip** Purchase an inexpensive handheld mandolin slicer to make thin cuts easier and more uniform; just be careful because those blades are sharp! You might want to use cut-resistant gloves, which are handy when using a mandolin.

Quick-Pickled Red Onions

Makes about 1 cup

1 cup unseasoned rice vinegar or white wine vinegar

1 cup water

2 teaspoons kosher salt

1 medium red onion, halved and thinly sliced into half-moons

In a medium saucepan, bring the vinegar, water and salt to a boil. Place the onions in a glass or ceramic bowl and pour the hot vinegar mixture over them. Cover and soak for 10 to 15 minutes before using, reserving the liquid for storage. Use a fork to scoop out the onions, leaving the liquid behind.

To store, transfer to a covered glass jar, with enough of the pickling liquid to reach the top of the onions. Keep in the refrigerator for up to a week.

 **notes**

I prefer these super tangy without any added sugar, but add a tablespoon of brown sugar to the vinegar as it warms if you want to temper the tanginess.

SMART tip: There's no older trick in a Mom's handbook than putting out a plate of raw veggies with ranch dressing. You'll get picky eaters to clear a plate of crudités in no time.

Homemade Buttermilk Ranch Dressing

Makes 2 cups

- 1 cup good-quality mayonnaise
- ½ cup well-shaken buttermilk
- 1½ tablespoons fresh lemon juice
- ½ cup plain Greek yogurt (nonfat, whole milk or anything in between)
- ½ teaspoon onion powder
- ½ teaspoon garlic powder
- 1½ teaspoons kosher salt
- 1 tablespoon minced fresh chives
- 1 tablespoon minced fresh flat-leaf parsley
- 1 tablespoon minced fresh mint leaves

In a food processor or high-powered blender, add the mayo, buttermilk, lemon juice, yogurt, onion powder, garlic powder and salt. Pulse to combine using on/off bursts. Check the consistency. If you'd like to thin out the dressing for salad, add a couple more tablespoons of buttermilk. Taste for seasoning and acidity; adjust with more salt or lemon juice.

Add the herbs and pulse in a couple of quick on/off bursts a few more times to combine. Cover and refrigerate for up to 1 week.

Serve on a crisp iceberg wedge or baby gem salad, or over a chef's salad of butter lettuce, diced ham, diced or grated Swiss cheese, hard-boiled eggs, shredded carrots and chopped tomatoes.

Variations: Add a chopped jalapeño, seeds removed, to make a spicy version. When I do this, I replace the parsley with cilantro and omit the mint.

To make blue cheese dressing, mix in 6 ounces crumbled blue cheese (about 1½ cups), preferably from a wedge instead of pre-crumbled.

For feta dressing, mix in 6 ounces crumbled feta (about 1½ cups) from a block stored in brine. I prefer sheep's milk feta from Israel, Greece or France.

notes

Ingredients make a big difference in the outcome of this dressing, so use good-quality mayonnaise such as Hellman's, Best Foods or Duke's. If you overprocess the dressing after you add the herbs, it will turn green but still taste great. I sometimes substitute chopped green onions (green part only) for the chives.

 **SMART tip** This dressing is good with mixed greens, mild butter lettuce, arugula or spinach. Use up leftover fresh herbs, such as chives, mint or parsley, in the salad mix for a fresh, bright flavor.

Super Simple Salad Dressing

Makes about 1 cup, enough for 3 or 4 family-size salads

¼ cup apple cider vinegar

1 heaping tablespoon minced shallot (about ½ small shallot)

1 teaspoon Dijon mustard or grainy German-style mustard

½ cup extra virgin olive oil

½ teaspoon kosher salt

Freshly ground black pepper

Place the vinegar and shallots in a small glass jar with a tight-fitting lid. Let sit for 10 minutes so the shallots marinate in the vinegar and lose their sharp, raw flavor. (This is an important step that makes a difference in the final flavor outcome.)

Add the mustard, olive oil, salt and pepper to the container, seal tightly and shake well to combine. Taste and adjust the seasoning if necessary. Keep covered in the refrigerator for up to 2 weeks. Bring the dressing to room temperature and shake well before tossing with salad greens.

Variations: Use 1 teaspoon minced garlic instead of the shallot. Try champagne vinegar or lemon juice instead of apple cider vinegar. Or use balsamic vinegar and add about a teaspoon of honey for a touch of sweetness.

notes

To taste for flavor, you can't just scoop up a spoonful of dressing and know what your salad will taste like. Dip a lettuce leaf into the dressing and try it. That way, you'll get an accurate idea of what your finished salad will taste like. Adjust with more olive oil to mellow out the tartness, or more salt or pepper. Note that extra virgin olive oil will sometimes solidify in the refrigerator, but it's still good! When it comes back to room temperature, it will liquefy.

Meatless Mains

As a way to sneak in more vegetables and cut down on our meat intake, I include a veggie-based dinner in my meal plan at least once a week.

There are no complaints from my people when there's a carb like pasta or rice mixed in with the veggies. Note that even though these dishes are meatless, they're adaptable for adding shredded rotisserie chicken, ground meat or chopped leftover meat.

When cooking pasta, be sure to add about a tablespoon of kosher salt per gallon of water. Most of it ends up down the drain, but it helps flavor the cooked pasta, and some of that starchy and salty pasta water can help finish and bring together the finished sauce.

46 Cherry Tomato Confit with Elbow Pasta

48 "Any Greens" Pesto Pasta

50 Vegetable Bolognese Rigatoni

52 Pantry Pasta

54 No-Boil Spinach Lasagna

56 Healthy Eggplant Parmesan with Pomodoro Sauce

60 Summer Farro "Risotto"

62 Spicy Udon Noodles

64 Peanut Noodles

66 Egg Roll in a Bowl

68 Aunt Shelley's Fried Rice

70 Chana Masala

72 Instant Pot Black-Eyed Peas and Greens

SMART tip: Once the tomatoes are cooked, any leftover olive oil and garlic can be stored in a glass container in the fridge and used for tomato-based pasta dishes.

Cherry Tomato Confit with Elbow Pasta

Serves 4 to 6

- 3 cups small red or multicolor cherry or Sweet 100 tomatoes
- 4 garlic cloves, smashed and peeled
- ½ cup extra virgin olive oil
- 4 fresh thyme sprigs
- 4 fresh oregano sprigs
- 1 teaspoon kosher salt
- 6 fresh basil leaves, thinly sliced crosswise
- 1 pound elbow pasta, cooked al dente and drained or pasta of choice
- Coarse salt

Preheat the oven to 375 degrees.

In an 8-inch round or square baking dish, add the tomatoes, garlic, olive oil, thyme, oregano and kosher salt. Bake for 40 to 45 minutes, until the tomatoes are golden and bubbly. Remove from the oven and discard thyme and oregano stems.

In a large serving bowl, use a slotted spoon to add the tomatoes. Add the basil and elbow pasta and gently toss. Finish with a sprinkle of coarse salt and serve.

You can also serve these tomatoes as an appetizer with a side of chèvre, burrata or feta cheese and a sliced baguette. Or try serving them over Creamy Hands-Off Polenta (page 166).

notes

The cooked tomatoes can also be used as a topping for crostini or on grilled salmon or chicken. It might seem like a lot of olive oil, but you need enough for the tomatoes to be poached. Top the pasta with freshly grated parmesan if you prefer.

 **SMART tip** The pesto can be stored in the refrigerator for about a week. Add a thin layer of olive oil on top to keep it from oxidizing.

"Any Greens" Pesto Pasta

Serves 4 to 6

¼ cup pecans, pistachios, walnuts, almonds or pine nuts

½ cup freshly grated Parmigiano-Reggiano, pecorino or Grana Padano cheese (about 2 ounces)

3 cups packed leafy greens (basil, spinach, arugula, kale, Swiss chard, carrot tops, flat-leaf parsley or a combination)

1 garlic clove, smashed and peeled

2 tablespoons fresh lemon juice

½ teaspoon kosher or coarse salt

Freshly ground black pepper

½ to ¾ cup extra virgin olive oil, more or less depending on how thick you like your pesto

1 pound cavatappi pasta, cooked al dente and drained or pasta of your choice

In a food processor, add the nuts, cheese, greens, garlic and lemon juice. Season with salt and pepper. Pulse in quick on/off bursts until the mixture is finely chopped but not completely pureed, 15 to 20 times. Scrape down the bowl and pulse again if necessary.

In the feed tube in the top of the food processor, add the olive oil and pulse, being careful not to overpuree or completely blend the pesto. Taste for seasoning and add more salt and pepper if needed.

In a large bowl, toss the pesto with the cavatappi.

notes

Trust me, you can use any greens for this—I've made countless variations to use up odds and ends in my refrigerator and garden. You can also use the pesto on paninis or caprese sandwiches, or stir some into vegetable soup as a type of pistou.

 **SMART tip** Cleaning leeks well is important. Cut them in half lengthwise, to the root, but not completely through the root so they stay attached. Place them under running water and open up the layers of the leek to rinse out any sand.

Vegetable Bolognese Rigatoni

Serves 4 to 6

- 3 tablespoons extra virgin olive oil
- 1 leek (white and light green parts), chopped
- ½ yellow onion, chopped
- 3 garlic cloves, minced (about 1 tablespoon)
- 1 medium carrot, sliced (no need to peel)
- 1 celery stalk, sliced
- 5 ounces shiitake mushrooms, stems removed, sliced
- 8 ounces Baby Bella or button mushrooms, sliced
- 1 teaspoon kosher salt
- ½ teaspoon fresh thyme leaves, chopped
- ½ cup red wine
- 1 tablespoon tomato paste
- 1 (28-ounce) can crushed tomatoes
- ¼ teaspoon crushed red pepper flakes
- Freshly ground black pepper
- ¼ cup freshly grated Parmigiano-Reggiano or pecorino cheese (optional)
- 16 ounces rigatoni, cooked al dente and drained

In a large high-sided sauté pan, heat the olive oil. Add the leeks, onions, garlic, carrots, celery, mushrooms, salt and thyme. Cook for 7 to 8 minutes, stirring occasionally, until the vegetables are fragrant and softened. Transfer the vegetables to a food processor and pulse in on/off bursts until vegetables are in small pieces but not pureed. Set aside.

Return the empty pan to the stove over medium heat and add the red wine, scraping up any browned vegetables. Simmer the wine for 3 to 4 minutes, until slightly reduced. Add back the vegetables, the tomato paste, crushed tomatoes, red pepper flakes and black pepper and stir. Cook for about 15 minutes to let the flavors come together.

Remove from the heat and stir in the cheese, if using. Serve tossed with rigatoni.

You can also serve the sauce over pappardelle, tortellini, ravioli or Creamy Hands-Off Polenta (page 166).

notes

Mushrooms add a filling, meaty texture and tons of umami flavor. If you can't find shiitake mushrooms, use extra button mushrooms. I promise you won't notice the meat is missing.

 Homemade breadcrumbs are easy and delicious. Use a leftover baguette or loaf of stale crusty bread. Cut it into cubes and toast in a 400-degree oven until golden. Pulse in a food processor to make fine breadcrumbs. Store in an airtight container in the freezer for up to 3 months.

Pantry Pasta

Serves 4

- 8 ounces spaghetti
- 1 tablespoon kosher salt
- ¼ cup extra virgin olive oil
- 4 garlic cloves, thinly sliced
- ¼ teaspoon crushed red pepper flakes
- 4 tablespoons butter or extra virgin olive oil
- Freshly ground black pepper
- ¼ cup plain breadcrumbs, lightly toasted in a nonstick skillet
- ¾ cup freshly grated Parmigiano-Reggiano cheese, plus more for serving
- Coarse salt

Cook the spaghetti in salted water. When al dente, reserve 1 cup of the pasta water, drain and set aside.

In a large heavy skillet over medium heat, heat the olive oil. Add the garlic and stir occasionally until golden, 1 to 2 minutes. Turn the heat down to low, add the red pepper flakes and cook about 30 seconds. Carefully add the reserved pasta water and stir for about 1 minute.

Add the spaghetti, butter, lots of black pepper and the breadcrumbs. Using tongs, gently toss to combine, about 4 minutes. (The sauce will thicken and coat the spaghetti.) Add the parmesan and stir to combine. Finish with salt and serve immediately with extra cheese on the side.

notes

If you have any fresh herbs on hand, like parsley, oregano or basil, you can chop and add to the pan with the parmesan. Or you could add a couple of handfuls of chopped spinach, kale or arugula leaves when you add the breadcrumbs.

SMART tip: The genius of this recipe is that you don't need to boil the pasta sheets. To squeeze the spinach dry, put it in a clean kitchen towel that you don't mind dying green. Squeeze well and let the water drain out.

No-Boil Spinach Lasagna

Serves 8

---

1 (15-ounce) container ricotta cheese

10 ounces frozen chopped spinach, thawed and squeezed dry

¼ cup milk (skim, 2% or whole)

1 egg

1 cup freshly grated Parmigiano-Reggiano cheese, divided

1 teaspoon kosher salt

Freshly ground black pepper

A few gratings of nutmeg

5½ cups Pomodoro Sauce (page 56) or store-bought tomato sauce

8 ounces no-boil lasagna noodles (about 12 noodles)

1 cup grated part-skim mozzarella cheese

Thinly sliced basil or chopped flat-leaf parsley, for serving

---

Preheat the oven to 350 degrees.

In a medium bowl, combine the ricotta, spinach, milk, egg, ¾ cup of the parmesan, salt, pepper and nutmeg.

In a 9×13-inch ceramic or glass baking dish, spread 1 cup of the sauce to cover the bottom. Top with a single layer of noodles without overlapping them. Spread on top of the noodles ⅓ of the spinach-ricotta mixture, then another cup of sauce. Add two more layers of noodles, spinach-ricotta mixture and sauce. Top with a final layer of noodles, the remaining sauce, the mozzarella and ¼ cup parmesan. Be sure the top layer of noodles is covered with sauce. (If any edges are uncovered, they will be crispy instead of soft.)

Bake uncovered for 50 minutes in the middle of the oven, until bubbly and golden brown. If the parmesan starts to get too brown, cover the pan with foil. Remove from the oven and let stand for about 10 minutes before cutting. If you'd like to add a touch of green on top before serving, garnish with basil or flat-leaf parsley.

notes

Instead of grated mozzarella, you can use an 8-ounce ball of fresh mozzarella, cut into 8 slices. Or if you want this heartier, add a pound of cooked crumbled mild Italian sausage layered on top of the spinach-ricotta mixture.

SMART tip: Leftover sauce freezes perfectly, so make a double batch and stash some for a future dinner. Pair this with crusty bread or simple pasta to mop up the delicious extra sauce in the pan.

Healthy Eggplant Parmesan with Pomodoro Sauce

Serves 4

Pomodoro Sauce

½ cup extra virgin olive oil

2 medium shallots, sliced, about ⅓ cup

4 garlic cloves, smashed

1 carrot, sliced (no need to peel)

1 (28-ounce) can whole peeled tomatoes, with their juice

½ teaspoon kosher salt

4 tablespoons unsalted butter, optional

In a medium saucepan, heat the olive oil over medium heat. It may seem like a lot of oil, but good-quality olive oil makes a difference in the finished sauce. Add the shallots and garlic and cook, stirring often, until slightly golden, about 1-2 minutes. Add the carrots and cook for another minute. Stir in the tomatoes and salt. Simmer, covered, on medium heat until the vegetables are softened, 15 to 20 minutes.

Puree in the saucepan with an immersion blender, or carefully transfer to a blender in batches to puree. Taste for seasoning and add more salt if desired. Keep the heat on low and stir in the butter until melted and incorporated into the sauce. If you're watching your cholesterol, you can skip the butter, but it rounds out the flavor of the sauce. Remove from the heat and set aside.

Continued on next page.

notes

If you're in a hurry, just use good-quality store-bought tomato sauce. My favorite brand is Rao's Homemade Marinara sauce.

Eggplant Parmesan

2 medium eggplants roughly the same width, or 3-4 small globe eggplants, about 3 pounds

Kosher salt

3 tablespoons extra virgin olive oil

4 cups Pomodoro Sauce

1 (8-ounce) ball fresh mozzarella, cut into 12 slices

½ to 1 cup freshly grated Parmigiano-Reggiano cheese

12 large fresh basil leaves, plus more for serving

Coarse salt

Slice the eggplants into 12 ½-inch rounds. Place them on a sheet pan and salt both sides generously. (Be sure to salt the eggplant well since it helps to draw out excess moisture and enhance the flavor.) After 30 minutes, use a paper towel to remove the salt and pat dry both sides of the eggplant slices. Brush both sides with olive oil.

Preheat a grill pan or outdoor grill to medium-high and preheat the oven to 400 degrees.

Working in batches if necessary, grill the eggplant for 2 to 3 minutes per side, until softened but still holding their shape. Transfer the slices to a platter.

In a 9×13-inch ceramic baking dish, spread 1½ cups of the sauce. On top lay 6 rounds of eggplant. Top each with a slice of mozzarella, a teaspoon of parmesan, a couple of tablespoons of sauce and a basil leaf. Add another layer of eggplant, mozzarella, parmesan, the remaining sauce and basil leaves. If you have a little extra sauce, just add it to the baking dish around the stacked eggplant rounds. Bake until the cheeses are melted and everything is warm throughout, 25-30 minutes. Top with thinly sliced basil leaves and a sprinkling of coarse salt.

notes

To make this dairy-free, omit the cheeses and just use tomato sauce—you'll have a "parmesan-free" eggplant parm. Add an extra sprinkle of kosher salt since parmesan is salty and you're leaving it out. I don't love the flavor of nutritional yeast, but you could use it sparingly instead of the parmesan as a substitute.

SMART tip: If you want to serve this during the week, you can roast the vegetables on the weekend and keep them refrigerated for up to 4 days.

Summer Farro "Risotto"

Serves 4

- 1 large zucchini, trimmed and diced
- 1 large eggplant, skin on, trimmed and diced
- 2 cups cherry tomatoes, halved
- 4 tablespoons extra virgin olive oil, divided
- ½ teaspoon kosher salt
- 1 yellow or red onion, diced
- 2 garlic cloves, minced
- 1 cup uncooked pearled farro
- 4 cups chicken stock, vegetable stock or water
- 2 tablespoons unsalted butter
- ¼ cup freshly grated Parmigiano-Reggiano or pecorino cheese
- 2 tablespoons fresh basil or flat-leaf parsley
- Freshly ground black pepper

Garnish: Chopped fresh parsley or basil; extra virgin olive oil; additional Parmigiano-Reggiano

Preheat the oven to 400 degrees.

On a half sheet pan, add the zucchini, eggplant and cherry tomatoes in a pile. Drizzle with 2 tablespoons of the olive oil and toss to coat. Spread out the vegetables in a single layer and sprinkle with the salt. Roast for 30 minutes, until softened and golden. Remove from the oven and set aside.

In a large skillet over medium-high heat, warm the remaining 2 tablespoons of olive oil. Add the onions and cook for about 3 minutes, until softened. Add the garlic and cook for 2 more minutes. Add the farro and cook, just long enough to coat the farro with the onions and garlic. Pour in the chicken stock and bring to a low boil. Once the stock starts to boil, reduce heat to medium. Cook uncovered, stirring occasionally, for 40 minutes, until the farro has absorbed the liquid and is softened. Taste the farro for doneness after about 15 minutes since some quick-cooking varieties will absorb liquid faster. If the farro starts to stick to the pan, add ¼ cup stock or water to loosen it up.

Add the roasted vegetables to the farro and stir to combine. Add the butter and parmesan and stir until melted. Taste for seasoning and adjust with more salt and pepper if desired. Spoon into bowls and garnish with herbs, a drizzle of extra virgin olive oil and additional parmesan cheese.

notes

To keep it vegan, use vegetable stock or water and olive oil instead of butter; omit the parmesan.

In winter, replace zucchini and eggplant with a chopped fennel bulb and 2 cups cauliflower florets.

SMART tip To make your prep faster, use a 16-ounce bag of store-bought shredded cabbage.

Spicy Udon Noodles

Serves 6-8

- 5 tablespoons low-sodium soy sauce, tamari or coconut aminos
- 3 tablespoons unseasoned rice vinegar
- 1 tablespoon plus 1 teaspoon toasted or regular sesame oil
- 1 tablespoon kosher salt, for cooking the udon noodles
- 9-10 ounces udon noodles
- ½ small green cabbage or Napa cabbage, thinly sliced
- 2 carrots, grated (no need to peel)
- 1 red bell pepper, thinly sliced
- ¼ cup avocado oil
- 5 teaspoons sesame seeds
- 2 teaspoons red pepper flakes, or less to tone down the spice
- 10 green onions (white and green parts), thinly sliced

Garnish: Sliced green onions (green parts); sesame seeds

In a small bowl, whisk together soy sauce, rice vinegar and sesame oil. Set aside.

Bring a large pot of salted water to a boil. Add the noodles and cook until al dente by following the package instructions. While the noodles are cooking, place the sliced vegetables in a large colander in the sink. When the noodles are ready, pour the hot water and noodles directly over the vegetables in the colander. The hot water will soften the vegetables and the noodles will end up on top, so make sure there's enough room to accommodate them before draining.

In a large wok or the same large pot you used to cook the udon noodles, heat the oil over medium heat. Add the sesame seeds and red pepper flakes. Cook until the red pepper flakes become fragrant and start to toast, about 2 minutes, being careful not to burn the sesame seeds. Stir in the green onions and the soy sauce mixture. Add the cooked noodles and vegetables from the colander and use tongs to toss well to combine. The cabbage will wilt and soften as you warm everything together. Finish with additional green onions and sesame seeds and serve.

notes

Udon noodles are a Japanese wheat noodle perfect for soups or stir fries. They may come in slightly different widths or in round or rectangular shapes; any variety of plain udon works great. Leftovers are amazing for cold lunches during the week!

SMART tip: You may want to make a double batch of this recipe because everyone will want seconds, and leftovers are delicious for a cold weekday lunch!

Peanut Noodles

Serves 4

- 1 tablespoon avocado oil
- 2 garlic cloves, minced
- 1 teaspoon sriracha
- 1 tablespoon tomato paste
- ½ cup water
- ½ teaspoon sugar
- 2 tablespoons creamy or crunchy peanut butter
- ¼ cup hoisin sauce
- 8 ounces Canton-style egg noodles or spaghetti, cooked al dente and drained

Garnish: ¼ cup unsalted toasted peanuts, chopped; 2 green onions (green parts only), thinly sliced; jalapeño chiles, chopped

In a small saucepan over medium-low heat, heat the avocado oil. Add the garlic, sriracha and tomato paste. Fry until the garlic is golden but not burnt, about 1-2 minutes. Add the water, sugar, peanut butter and hoisin sauce and whisk to combine. Bring to a simmer, reduce the heat and cook for 2 to 3 minutes, until slightly thickened. Remove from the heat.

In a medium serving bowl, toss the peanut sauce with noodles. Garnish with the peanuts, green onions and jalapeños and serve.

notes

Instead of sriracha, I also like to use Korean gochujang chili paste, which you can find with the Asian condiments at most grocery stores.

 **SMART tip** Be sure to prep all the vegetables before you start cooking—it goes fast!

Egg Roll in a Bowl

Serves 4 to 6

¼ cup low-sodium soy sauce, tamari or coconut aminos, plus more for serving

2 teaspoons unseasoned rice vinegar

2 teaspoons toasted or regular sesame oil

1 tablespoon avocado oil

½ yellow or white onion, thinly sliced into half-moons

2 garlic cloves, minced

2 teaspoons finely grated fresh ginger (no need to peel)

3 cups packed thinly sliced napa or green cabbage (about ½ head)

2 cups thinly sliced bok choy (green and white parts)

1 cup shredded carrots (store-bought, or 1-2 carrots shredded on a box grater)

4 ounces shiitake mushrooms, stems removed, sliced

Garnish: 1 green onion (white and green parts), thinly sliced; sesame seeds; fresh cilantro, chopped; sriracha or Asian chili sauce

In a small bowl, mix the soy sauce, rice vinegar and sesame oil. Set aside.

Preheat a large high-sided skillet or wok over medium-high heat. Heat the avocado oil and add the onions. Cook until softened and slightly golden, 2 to 3 minutes. Add the garlic and ginger and cook for about a minute. Add the cabbage, bok choy, carrots and mushrooms. Stir to combine. (You will have a lot of veggies, so stir carefully.) Turn the heat to low and cover the pan so the vegetables cook down quickly, stirring occasionally, 10 to 15 minutes.

Add the soy sauce mixture and stir to combine. Taste for seasoning; sometimes I add one more splash of soy sauce. Serve warm with garnish of your choice and an extra dash of soy sauce.

notes

While not traditional in any way, this deconstructed egg roll stir fry is packed with vegetables and relatively quick. Cremini or button mushrooms work if you can't find shiitakes. This is also delicious with a pound of ground pork or chicken added to the mix. Cook the meat after the onion; drain off any fat and leave the meat in the pan as you add the other ingredients.

 **SMART tip** This is a great way to use up leftover cooked vegetables, cooked beef, pork or chicken and take-out white rice. Slightly dried-out rice actually works great because it won't clump together in the pan.

Aunt Shelley's Fried Rice

Serves 4 to 6

3 tablespoons avocado oil, divided

1 yellow onion, chopped

6 green onions (white and green parts), sliced

5 celery stalks, chopped

2 or 3 carrots, chopped (no need to peel), or about 1 cup packaged shredded carrots

3 to 4 cups cooked short-grain sushi rice (Cal-Rose or Nishiki, from 1½ cups uncooked)

3 tablespoons toasted or regular sesame oil

¼ cup low-sodium soy sauce, tamari or coconut aminos

4 cups chopped mixed green vegetables (such as broccoli, asparagus, sugar snap peas, green beans or bok choy)

4 eggs, whisked

Garnish: Sriracha or sambal oelek; sliced green onions (green part)

In a large Dutch oven or wok over medium heat, heat 2 tablespoons avocado oil. Add the yellow and green onions and celery; cook until softened, about 4 minutes. Add carrots and cook for a minute more.

Add the rice to the pan, but before stirring it in, sprinkle it with the sesame oil, which helps to flavor it. Add the soy sauce and mix well to combine. Be sure to scrape up the onions and celery on the bottom of the pan. Add the green vegetables and cook until softened. Remove from the heat and set aside.

In a nonstick pan over medium heat, warm the remaining 1 tablespoon avocado oil. Add the eggs and push them gently across the pan to create long ribbons of scrambled eggs.

Once the eggs are cooked, add them to the rice and fold them in to combine. Taste for seasoning and add more soy sauce if necessary. Garnish with sriracha, sambal oelek or sliced green onions.

notes

My husband's aunt, Shelley Yim, always makes this on Christmas morning with leftover beef from Christmas Eve dinner. It's way more delicious for sleepy Christmas mornings, in my humble opinion, than coffee cake.

SMART tip: Add 2 cups small cauliflower florets or spinach leaves when you add the garbanzos to stretch the recipe to feed more people and pack in more veggies.

Chana Masala

Serves 4

- 2 teaspoons ground coriander
- 1 teaspoon ground cumin
- 1 teaspoon paprika
- ½ teaspoon ground turmeric
- ¼ teaspoon cayenne pepper
- 3 tablespoons avocado oil
- 1 yellow onion, chopped
- 1 teaspoon cumin seeds
- 4 garlic cloves, minced
- 1 small green chile (such as serrano, jalapeño or Thai), sliced
- 2 teaspoons finely grated ginger (no need to peel)
- 2 cups plus 1 tablespoon water
- 2 medium tomatoes, chopped
- 2 cans (15-ounces each) garbanzo beans, drained and rinsed
- 1½ teaspoons kosher salt
- Fresh lemon juice, chopped fresh cilantro, steamed basmati rice, for serving
- **Garnish:** Sliced green onions (green part); sriracha or sambal oelek

In a small bowl, combine the coriander, cumin, paprika, turmeric and cayenne. Set aside.

Heat a large heavy-bottomed skillet over medium-high heat. Once hot, add the avocado oil, onion and cumin seeds. Cook for 4 to 5 minutes, until golden. Add the garlic, chile and ginger and sauté for another 2 to 3 minutes. Deglaze the pan with 1 tablespoon water, if needed. Add the spice mixture. Continue to cook over medium heat for 1-2 minutes to bloom and roast the spices. Give the mixture a few stirs, then add the tomatoes and garbanzos, salt and 2 cups water. Bring to a low boil. Cover, reduce the heat to low and cook for 25 to 30 minutes, until the garbanzos are tender.

Uncover and use a spoon or potato masher to slightly crush some of the garbanzos to thicken the stew and bring together the flavors. Stir in salt, lemon juice and cilantro, taste and adjust if necessary. Serve with rice and your choice of garnish.

notes

This recipe has been adapted from my friend Izzah from *Tea for Turmeric*. Head to her blog for healthy and approachable South Asian recipes. Ginger doesn't really need to be peeled; just wash it well. If you prefer to peel it, use the side of a small spoon to scrape off the skin. And I use a Microplane to grate the ginger, which creates a fine paste.

SMART tip Don't stress about measuring the greens—just grab two big handfuls, which should equal about 2 cups.

Instant Pot Black-Eyed Peas and Greens

Serves 4 to 6

1 pound dried black-eyed peas

6 cups water

2 tablespoons extra virgin olive oil

1 trimmed fennel bulb, halved and cored, then chopped

1 leek, chopped (white and light green parts)

2 garlic cloves, minced

1 teaspoon kosher salt

4 cups chicken stock or water

1 can (15-ounces) fire-roasted crushed tomatoes

2 big handfuls spinach or Swiss chard leaves, roughly chopped

Freshly ground black pepper

Steamed rice or cooked quinoa and hot sauce (such as Crystal or Tabasco), for serving

Add the dried black-eyed peas and water to the stainless-steel insert of an Instant Pot. Seal the lid and valve and set to *Manual/High* for 4 minutes. Let the pressure release naturally.

Drain the black-eyed peas in a colander and wipe out the Instant Pot insert with a paper towel. Add the olive oil and heat on the *Sauté* setting. Add the fennel, leek and garlic and cook until the vegetables are softened. Add the salt, chicken stock, tomatoes and the black-eyed peas and stir. Seal the lid and pressure valve and set to the *Bean/Chili* setting for 10 minutes. Manually release the pressure. Stir in the spinach and seal the lid. Let sit on the *Keep Warm* setting for 2 to 3 minutes, to wilt the spinach. Taste for salt and pepper. Serve in bowls over steamed rice with a dash or two of Louisiana-style hot sauce.

notes

Instead of black-eyed peas, you can use small white cannellini or Great Northern beans. If you have ham left over, you can chop it and add it when you add the greens.

Fish

Cooking fish at home shouldn't feel intimidating.

With a few tips for selecting good fish, knowing the internal temperature of fish when it's cooked through (145 degrees on an instant-read thermometer) and some delicious sauces, you'll have restaurant-quality fish at home in no time. And don't be afraid of frozen fish—you can find great flash-frozen fish that's high quality. I like to stock my freezer with frozen wild cod and salmon. For cooking, I tend to prefer high heat and short times, usually 7 to 10 minutes, although slow-roasting cuts of fattier fish like salmon and arctic char creates a texture that's melty and moist.

Parchment paper is your friend—don't be afraid to roast any type of fish in parchment paper packets for delicious, flaky fish. See page 84 to learn how. Sauces are also your friends. I was always in charge of making the tartar sauce when I was a little girl—my version is on page 95. But now I prefer a Spicy Rémoulade (page 94) or zesty green Chermoula (page 95).

You won't find any shellfish recipes in this chapter—unfortunately, I have an allergy. I don't miss any of it except shrimp. You'll have to have some for me instead.

78
Panko-Crusted Fish Sticks

80
Browned Butter and Basil Trout

82
Halibut Poached in Lemon and White Wine

84
Parchment Paper Fish Packets
(Fish en Papillote)

86
Red Snapper Roasted with Italian Salsa Verde

88
Sockeye Salmon with Haricots Verts and Cherry Tomatoes

90
Blackened Redfish Tacos

92
Fish Sauces

94-95
Spicy Rémoulade

Chipotle-Lime Crema

Chermoula

Tartar Sauce

SMART tip: If you don't have a roasting rack, use a wire cooling rack. Or cook these directly on parchment paper, but keep in the mind that the bottom of the fish sticks won't get as crispy.

Panko-Crusted Fish Sticks

Serves 4

1 egg
1¾ cups unseasoned panko
1 tablespoon plus 1 teaspoon Cajun seasoning (such as Tony Chachere's)
¼ teaspoon kosher salt
1½-2 pounds wild Alaskan cod, cut into 3-inch strips
Lemon wedges and Spicy Rémoulade (page 94) or Tartar Sauce (page 95), for serving
Garnish: Fresh parsley, chopped

Move a rack to the top third in the oven. Preheat the oven to 400 degrees. Line a half sheet pan with parchment paper and top with a roasting rack.

In a shallow bowl, whisk the egg; set aside. In another shallow bowl, mix the panko, 1 tablespoon of the Cajun seasoning and the salt. Dip the cod pieces in the egg, then roll in the panko mixture, pressing lightly to adhere. Place the coated fish sticks on the rack, not touching.

Bake in the upper third of the oven for about 5 minutes. Using a spatula or tongs, carefully turn the fish sticks. Bake until lightly browned, about 5 more minutes. The internal temperature should register 145 degrees on an instant-read thermometer.

Serve the fish sticks with lemon wedges and rémoulade or tartar sauce and garnish with parsley if desired.

notes

To make this recipe gluten-free, use almond meal or your favorite gluten-free breadcrumbs. You may also find that some stores carry gluten-free panko.

SMART tip: If you heat a Pyrex baker over 450 degrees, it can shatter. So I don't use them over 400 degrees, to be safe. My oven is hard enough to clean as it is!

Browned Butter and Basil Trout

Serves 2

½ cup unsalted butter
Juice of ½ lemon
1 teaspoon kosher salt, plus more for seasoning the fish
Freshly ground black pepper, plus more for seasoning the fish
12 fresh basil leaves, thinly sliced crosswise, divided
1-2 skin-on trout fillets, about 1 pound (preferably steelhead, rainbow or ruby red trout)
Garnish: Coarse salt; reserved basil leaves

Preheat the oven to 375 degrees.

Place the butter in a baking dish that will be just large enough to hold the fillets. Heat in the oven until the butter is melted and browned in spots, 15 to 20 minutes.

Carefully remove the baking dish from the oven and increase the oven temperature to 450 degrees. Add the lemon juice, salt, pepper and half the basil to the melted butter. Gently place the trout, skin side down, in the butter sauce and top it with more freshly ground pepper and a sprinkling of kosher salt. Roast for 10 to 12 minutes, until the flesh is opaque. The butter will brown in spots.

Carefully remove the dish from the oven, being careful not to burn yourself with the hot butter.

Serve the trout topped with a spoonful of the brown butter sauce, a sprinkle of the reserved basil and salt. I love serving this with rice, crusty bread or roasted potatoes to soak up the butter sauce.

notes

If you can't find good trout, this is amazing with halibut, cod, sea bass or haddock. If cooking thicker fillets, roast for 12 to 14 minutes, until the internal temperature is 145 degrees. I've used 2 teaspoons of fresh thyme leaves instead of the basil and it's equally delicious.

 **SMART tip** Don't be afraid to buy frozen fish; fish are often flash-frozen at the source where they're caught. Look for wild-caught frozen fillets that are individually vacuum sealed.

Halibut Poached in Lemon and White Wine

Serves 2

½ cup dry white wine (such as sauvignon blanc or chenin blanc)
2 (6-ounce) skin-on or skinless halibut fillets
1 lemon (cut in half, one side sliced)
1 tablespoon extra virgin olive oil
¼ teaspoon kosher salt
1 tablespoon capers
Freshly ground black pepper
Fresh dill, for serving

Preheat the oven to 400 degrees.

In a small roasting pan or oven-safe skillet, add the wine and the fillets. Squeeze the halved lemon on top of the fish, drizzle with the olive oil, and sprinkle with salt and pepper. Arrange the lemon slices and capers in the pan. Roast in the middle of the oven until opaque, 10 to 12 minutes, or until internal temperature reaches 145 degrees. To serve, spoon some of the white wine-lemon sauce and capers on top of the fillets. Top with fresh dill. I also love this with Chermoula (page 95) on the side.

 **notes**
Capers come in a variety of sizes, from ¼-inch, about the size of a pea, to over ½-inch, about the size of an olive. You can also use large caper berries here, available online and at gourmet markets.

SMART tip — Look for parchment paper cooking bags to make this super easy or use pre-cut parchment paper sheets that you fold in half and crimp tightly around the edges.

Parchment Paper Fish Packets (Fish en Papillote)

Serves 4

---

4 (6-ounce) fish fillets, skin on or skinless (such as snapper, flounder, cod, grouper, halibut, salmon, arctic char or swordfish steaks—whatever looks best!)
Kosher salt and freshly ground black pepper
2 tablespoons extra virgin olive oil
1 lemon, quartered

"Any Greens" Pesto (page 48), chopped fresh herbs and coarse salt, for serving
Fillings: Shelled peas; cherry tomatoes; chopped fresh herbs such as basil, dill, chives or parsley; lemon slices; capers or caper berries; olives; haricots verts or thin green beans

---

Preheat the oven to 400 degrees. Place four 12×16-inch pieces of parchment paper or parchment paper cooking bags on a half sheet pan.

Divide the fish among the parchment paper. Sprinkle with salt and pepper, drizzle with olive oil and squeeze lemon juice on top. Top each fillet with your choice of toppings and a tablespoon of the pesto, or serve the pesto on the side.

Fold the parchment paper over everything to bring the edges together. Tightly fold and crimp the edges from one far corner to the other, sealing tightly to make packets.

Bake for 15 to 20 minutes, until an instant-read thermometer registers 145 degrees when inserted through the parchment paper into the fish.

Place each packet on a plate and cut open, being careful of any steam that's released. Sprinkle the fish with additional fresh herbs, lemon juice and coarse salt, if desired. Serve immediately.

This would also be delicious with Chermoula (page 95) or Italian Salsa Verde (page 86) instead of the pesto.

notes

Use almost any fish for this: Try salmon, trout, redfish or swordfish steaks. If the fillet is thin, check the fish after 7 minutes in the oven.

 **SMART tip** If you're feeding picky eaters, roast the fish without the herb topping. Just drizzle the fillets with a little olive oil, lemon juice and salt, and roast.

Red Snapper Roasted with Italian Salsa Verde

Serves 6

- 2 cups minced fresh flat-leaf parsley (leaves and stems), about 1 large bunch
- 2 garlic cloves, grated on a Microplane
- 1 tablespoon capers, finely chopped
- 1 teaspoon caper juice
- 1 oil-packed anchovy fillet, finely chopped, or 1 teaspoon anchovy paste
- 2 teaspoons red wine vinegar
- 8 tablespoons extra virgin olive oil, divided
- ¼ teaspoon kosher salt
- Freshly ground black pepper
- 4 (6-ounce) skin-on red snapper or other white, flaky fish fillets
- Lemon wedges or slices and red pepper flakes, for serving

To make the salsa verde, combine in a small bowl the parsley, garlic, capers and juice, anchovy and red wine vinegar. Stir in 7 tablespoons of the olive oil, along with the salt and pepper. Set aside.

Preheat the oven to 425 degrees.

In a ceramic baking dish, drizzle the remaining tablespoon olive oil. Place the fish in the baking dish, skin side down. Top each fillet with about 2 tablespoons of the salsa verde. Set aside the remaining sauce.

Roast for 10 to 12 minutes, until the ends of each fillet flake easily. The internal temperature should register 145 degrees in an instant-read thermometer. If you're cooking a thicker fish such as halibut, you may have to add 5 minutes to the cooking time.

Transfer the fish to a platter or individual plates and serve with lemon and the remaining sauce on the side.

notes

Feel free to use any flaky fish in this recipe, such as halibut, sea bass or Texas redfish (also known as red drum). If you have extra Italian salsa verde, store leftovers in the refrigerator for up to 4 days to serve with roasted potatoes or chicken.

 **SMART tip** I prefer to roast a whole side of skin-on salmon. It's less likely to overcook and the presentation is pretty.

Sockeye Salmon with Haricots Verts and Cherry Tomatoes

Serves 6

One side of skin-on wild sockeye salmon, about 2-3 pounds
2 tablespoons extra virgin olive oil
½ teaspoon kosher salt
Freshly ground black pepper
Juice of 1 lemon
1 tablespoon capers
8 ounces haricots verts or thin green beans
1 cup cherry tomatoes
Lemon wedges or slices, for serving

Preheat the oven to 400 degrees. Line a half sheet pan with parchment paper.

Place the salmon skin side down in the middle of the prepared pan. Drizzle the olive oil on top. Sprinkle with salt and pepper, lemon juice and capers. Surround the fish with the haricots verts and tomatoes.

Roast in the middle of the oven until the flesh is opaque, about 7 minutes. Remove from the oven and serve with lemon.

If you'd like a sauce on the side, try this with Chermoula (page 95) or Spicy Rémoulade (page 94). If you have leftover salmon, make the Salmon Salad "Niçoise" (page 34) for a lunch or dinner later in the week.

notes

Try to source wild salmon—it's higher in omega-3 fatty acids than farmed salmon. But you can use almost any fish for this—try arctic char, halibut, trout, redfish or swordfish steaks; just check the internal temperature after 7 minutes and remove from the oven when it reaches 145 degrees.

SMART tip If you're short on time, it's okay to cheat by using store-bought blackened seasoning or Cajun seasoning such as Tony Chachere's. Or make a double batch of the homemade blackening spice for easier prep next time—and I promise if you make these, there will be a next time!

Blackened Redfish Tacos

Serves 4 to 6

1 tablespoon paprika
1½ teaspoons kosher salt
1 teaspoon onion powder
1 teaspoon garlic powder
¼ to ½ teaspoon cayenne pepper
½ teaspoon dried oregano
½ teaspoon dried thyme
Freshly ground black pepper
4 (6-ounce) skin-on redfish fillets
1 tablespoon extra virgin olive oil or fresh lime juice

Taco fixings: Corn or flour tortillas, warmed; shredded red or green cabbage; fresh cilantro leaves; fresh or pickled jalapeño slices; Quick-Pickled Red Onions (page 36); avocado slices; radish slices; lime wedges; hot sauce and salsa; Chipotle-Lime Crema (page 94)

Move a rack to the top third of the oven. Preheat the oven to 400 degrees. Line a sheet pan with parchment paper.

In a small bowl, mix together all the blackening spice ingredients; set aside.

Lay the fish fillets on the prepared pan and brush the top lightly with olive oil or lime juice to help the blackening spice adhere. Sprinkle the blackening spice generously over each fillet until well coated.

Roast in the oven for 10 minutes. Check the internal temperature; it should register 145 degrees on an instant-read thermometer.

To serve, flake the fish into warm tortillas with your toppings of choice.

These tacos are also delicious made with salmon or use the blackened seasoning for grilled chicken.

Fish Sauces

There's nothing like a tangy sauce to wake up simple roasted or grilled fish.

Try the spicy rémoulade with salmon, shrimp, crab cakes or fried pickles. It's also great mixed with canned tuna or as a spread for a turkey sandwich. Tartar sauce is the standard go-to. I've loved it since I was a kid and love it with lots of chopped cornichons; if you prefer, make it with sweet relish and skip the fresh herbs. Chermoula is a Moroccan herb sauce that's full of flavor from garlic, extra virgin olive oil and spices. Traditionally paired with fish, Chermoula can also be used with roasted lamb, chicken or grilled meats. Here's a quick tip: when cooking with cilantro and parsley, I also use the stems—they are tender and have just as much flavor as the leaves.

Top to Bottom: Chipotle-Lime Crema, Chermoula, Spicy Rémoulade, Tartar Sauce

Spicy Rémoulade

Makes about 1 cup

¾ cup good-quality mayonnaise (such as Hellman's, Best Foods or Duke's)
2 tablespoons Dijon mustard (grainy or smooth)
1 tablespoon fresh lemon juice
1 tablespoon Louisiana-style hot sauce (such as Crystal or Tabasco), or less to taste
2 garlic cloves, minced
2 teaspoons capers, drained and chopped
1 teaspoon Worcestershire sauce
1 teaspoon paprika
1 green onion (white and green parts), minced
¼ teaspoon kosher salt
⅛ teaspoon cayenne pepper or Cajun seasoning
1 tablespoon minced fresh flat-leaf parsley

In a small bowl, add the mayonnaise, mustard, lemon juice, hot sauce, garlic, capers, Worcestershire, paprika, green onion, salt and cayenne. Mix well to combine. Let sit for at least 30 minutes at room temperature so the flavors meld before serving.

If you're not planning to serve this right away, cover and store in the refrigerator. You can make this up to 3 days ahead, but it's best to stir in the parsley just before serving so it doesn't oxidize and turn brown.

Chipotle-Lime Crema

Makes about 1 cup

½ cup Mexican crema or sour cream
¼ cup good-quality mayonnaise (such as Hellman's, Best Foods or Duke's)
1½ teaspoons chipotle paste
¼ teaspoon garlic powder
Finely grated zest and juice of 1 lime
Kosher salt and freshly ground black pepper

In a medium bowl, combine the crema, mayonnaise, chipotle paste, garlic powder, lime zest and juice, and salt and pepper to taste. Stir well. Refrigerate, covered, until needed. This will keep for up to 4 days in the refrigerator.

I prefer chipotle paste in a tube because leftover paste can easily be stored in the refrigerator. You can use part of a can of chipotles in adobo sauce, finely chopped, instead of the paste; transfer the rest to a container with a tight-fitting lid and store in the refrigerator for up to a week or in the freezer for up to 3 months. If you don't have chipotles, you can also substitute a teaspoon of chipotle chile powder or a chili powder blend.

Chermoula

Makes about 1½ cups

5 garlic cloves, minced
2½ cups packed fresh flat-leaf parsley (leaves and stems)
2 cups packed fresh cilantro (leaves and stems)
Finely grated zest and juice of 1 lemon

1 teaspoon smoked or regular paprika
¼ teaspoon cayenne pepper, or more, to taste
2 teaspoons ground cumin
¾ teaspoon kosher salt
½ cup extra virgin olive oil

In a food processor or high-powered blender, add the garlic, parsley, cilantro, lemon zest and juice, paprika, cayenne pepper, cumin and salt. Pulse with on/off bursts to create a coarse mixture; don't process until smooth or pureed. With the machine running, add the oil in a steady stream until just combined. Taste for seasoning and add more lemon juice or salt if desired. Store in a tightly covered container in the refrigerator for 3 to 5 days.

Chermoula is the perfect condiment for fish, chicken or roasted vegetables. I also love it mixed into couscous, cooked white beans or vegetable soup.

Tartar Sauce

Makes about 2 cups

1 cup good-quality mayonnaise (such as Hellman's, Best Foods or Duke's)
1 cup finely chopped cornichons or dill pickles, or dill relish
1 tablespoon minced fresh dill or flat-leaf parsley
1 tablespoon fresh lemon juice

1 teaspoon Dijon mustard
¼ teaspoon kosher salt
Freshly ground black pepper
Optional additions: 1 tablespoon minced shallot or green onion; a few dashes of Tabasco or Crystal hot sauce; ½ teaspoon Old Bay seasoning

In a medium bowl, add the mayonnaise, pickles, herbs, lemon juice, Dijon mustard, salt and pepper. Stir well. Stir in one or more of the additions, if you like. (My kids didn't like the oniony addition when they were younger.) Taste and adjust the seasoning with salt or lemon juice, if necessary. Refrigerate, covered, until needed. Will keep for up to 4 days in the refrigerator.

Meaty Mains

My family loves any main dish that starts with ground meat.

It could be a simple pan of taco meat or ground chicken in lettuce cups (page 100) or a Quick Lamb Ragu (page 112). But I also love a slow cooked Pulled Pork (page 106) or French Dip Sandwich (page 120) or a great cut of meat on the grill (pages 114 and 116).

Grilling is easier than people realize. My four tips: Preheat the grill; brush down the grates after it's hot (path of least resistance, my friends); oil the grates, especially when grilling lean meats; and don't mess with or otherwise poke or prod what you're grilling. An instant-read thermometer is your best friend here. I've given meat cooking temperatures in all the grilling recipes.

Don't be afraid to ask the butcher for help when selecting meats; that's what they're for. They can spatchcock a chicken for you, trim meats and recommend a cut of meat or a substitution.

100 Ground Chicken in Lettuce Cups

102 Chicken Enchilada Casserole

104 Spatchcocked Chipotle-Lime Chicken

106 Dry-Rubbed Pulled Pork

108 Honey-Hoisin Pork Tenderloin

110 Slow Cooker Carnitas Tacos

112 Quick Lamb Ragu

114 Rosemary-Garlic Grilled Lamb Chops

116 Grilled Tri-Tip with Black Bean Sauce

118 Chile and Espresso–Rubbed Flank Steak

120 Slow Cooker French Dip Sandwiches

SMART tip: You can also use the rice vinegar-soy sauce mixture as a dumpling dipping sauce—add a pinch of red pepper flakes if you like spice.

Ground Chicken in Lettuce Cups

Serves 4-6

Rice Vinegar-Soy Sauce

¼ cup low-sodium soy sauce, tamari or coconut aminos

2 tablespoons unseasoned rice vinegar

1 tablespoon sugar (optional)

1½ teaspoons finely grated ginger (no need to peel)

1 teaspoon toasted or regular sesame oil

½ teaspoon minced garlic

Chicken

1 tablespoon avocado oil

1½ pounds ground dark meat chicken

8 green onions (white and green parts), sliced

2 carrots, diced (no need to peel)

8 ounces button or cremini mushrooms, chopped

½ cup low-sodium soy sauce, tamari or coconut aminos

2 tablespoons hoisin sauce

1 tablespoon finely grated ginger (no need to peel)

1 tablespoon water

2 teaspoons toasted or regular sesame oil

2 heads Bibb, iceberg or butter lettuce, washed, leaves separated but kept whole

Toppings (optional): Fresh cilantro leaves; sriracha; chopped peanuts

---

In a small bowl, add all the rice vinegar-soy sauce ingredients and mix well. Set aside.

In a large sauté pan over medium-high heat, heat the avocado oil. Add the chicken and cook, breaking it up into small pieces. When it's almost cooked through, add the green onions, carrots and mushrooms and cook for 3 to 4 minutes more, until meat is completely cooked through and carrots are softened.

In a small bowl, stir together the soy sauce, hoisin, ginger, water and sesame oil. Add to the chicken mixture, cover and simmer for about 5 minutes.

To assemble, top a lettuce leaf with a heaping ¼ cup of the chicken mixture and drizzle with 1 to 2 teaspoons of the rice vinegar-soy sauce. Add garnish of your choice and serve.

notes

This makes a large amount of chicken filling, but it's great for leftover lunches served over steamed rice.

 **SMART tip** If you use rotisserie chicken, this can be assembled in 15 minutes flat!

Chicken Enchilada Casserole

Serves 4

Avocado oil or cooking oil spray
1 (15-ounce) can red enchilada sauce
1 (8-ounce) can tomato sauce
3 (9-inch) flour or corn tortillas
2 cups shredded cooked chicken
1 (15-ounce) can pinto beans, drained and rinsed
1 cup shredded Monterey Jack or Mexican blend cheese
Avocado slices or chopped fresh cilantro, for serving

Preheat the oven to 350 degrees. Spray a pie dish or 9-inch cake pan with avocado oil or cooking spray.

In a wide shallow bowl, combine the enchilada sauce and tomato sauce. Spread ¼ cup of the sauce mixture on the bottom of the prepared pan. Dip a tortilla in the bowl of sauce to coat both sides; place the tortilla on the sauce in the bottom of the pan. Layer with half of the chicken and half of the pinto beans, then spread with another ¼ cup of the sauce. Top with another sauce-coated tortilla, the remaining chicken and pinto beans and another ¼ cup sauce. Coat the remaining tortilla in sauce, place it on top and top with any remaining sauce and the cheese.

Bake for 45 minutes. If the top gets too brown, cover with foil. Let stand for 5 minutes before serving.

notes

This has endless variations—layer in roasted corn, black beans or refried beans. Use cooked ground turkey, pork or beef instead of shredded chicken. I use Hatch Organic Red Enchilada Sauce or Siete Red Enchilada Sauce.

SMART tip: You can ask the butcher to spatchcock the chicken for you; be sure to ask for the spine. Freeze the spine for making chicken stock later.

Spatchcocked Chipotle-Lime Chicken

Serves 4

- 1 whole roasting chicken (3 to 3½ pounds)
- 1 bunch fresh cilantro, or parsley if you're not a cilantro fan
- 2 shallots, roughly chopped
- 2 garlic cloves, smashed and peeled
- 1 jalapeño chile, stem removed (no need to seed)
- 1 cup fresh orange juice
- ½ cup fresh lime juice
- 1 tablespoon chipotle paste or 1 chipotle chile in adobo sauce
- 1 tablespoon kosher salt
- Lime wedges or slices, for serving

To spatchcock the chicken, place the chicken on its breast on a cutting board and use sharp kitchen shears to cut along the right and left sides of the spine. Remove the spine and make a shallow cut in the middle of the breastbone on the rib side. Turn the chicken skin side up on the cutting board and press down on the breastbone so the chicken lies flat (you may hear it crack). You now have a spatchcocked chicken that will cook evenly.

In a high-powered blender, combine the cilantro, shallots, garlic, chile, orange juice, lime juice, chipotle paste and salt. Process the marinade to a puree.

Place the chicken in a stainless-steel or glass bowl and cover with the marinade, rotating the chicken to make sure it's well coated. Refrigerate for 3 hours or up to 8 hours. Note: There's no need to cover the chicken with plastic wrap, as long as nothing is touching the chicken and marinade, you're fine.

Preheat the oven to 425 degrees; use the convection roast setting if you have it. Remove the chicken from the marinade and place it on a roasting pan or on a parchment paper-lined half sheet pan. Make sure the chicken lies flat so the legs and wings are skin side up. Discard any remaining marinade. Roast for 45 minutes or until the internal temperature reaches 165 degrees.

Transfer the cooked chicken to a large carving board and let it rest for 5 minutes.

Pull off the wings and cut both leg and thigh portions off the chicken. (It's so easy to remove the legs because you're just cutting through the skin.) Cut the breast in half through the breastbone. You can then cut both the breast pieces in half again if you'd like to end up with 4 pieces of breast meat.

notes

You can simplify this by skipping the marinade. Just brush the skin with olive oil and sprinkle generously with kosher salt. Serve with lemon wedges on the side. I love to garnish platters with edible flowers from my garden, such as fennel flowers (shown here), purple mint flowers or white chive flowers.

SMART tip: If you like a "saucier" shredded pork, add a cup of your favorite jarred BBQ sauce to the slow cooker or Instant Pot when you add the meat.

Dry-Rubbed Pulled Pork

Serves 6

---

1 tablespoon paprika
1½ teaspoons onion powder
1½ teaspoons garlic powder
¼ to ½ teaspoon cayenne pepper
1½ teaspoons kosher salt
2 to 3 pounds bone-in or boneless pork shoulder
¼ cup water, for the Instant Pot version
Slider buns and cole slaw, for serving

In a small bowl, combine the spice mix ingredients. Pat the pork dry with a paper towel. If you're using boneless pork shoulder, cut it into 3 to 4 chunks. (This will help the meat shred more easily.) Rub the spices all over the pork.

Instant Pot Directions: Add the water to the base of the Instant Pot. Add the pork. Close the lid, seal the vent and cook on *High* pressure or *Meat/Stew* setting for 60 minutes. When the time is up, use a towel to cover the vent and turn it with tongs to release the steam. (Be very careful not to burn yourself.) When the steam has released, open the lid and shred the meat with two forks. If the meat doesn't shred easily, replace the lid, seal the vent and cook for another 15-20 minutes on *High* pressure or *Meat/Stew*. Carefully release the steam, open the lid and shred the meat. If there was a bone, remove it and discard.

Slow Cooker Directions: Add the seasoned pork to the slow cooker; no water is necessary in this version. Cover and cook on low for 6 to 7 hours. Check the meat after 6 hours, if it easily falls apart, remove the meat, shred it, and return it to the accumulated juices in the slow cooker. If the meat doesn't shred easily, return it to the slow cooker on *High* for another 45 to 60 minutes. If there was a bone, remove it and discard.

Serve on slider buns with coleslaw and pickles or in quesadillas with pickled jalapeños. Store extra shredded meat and any accumulated liquid for up to 4 days in the refrigerator.

notes

If you're short on time, sprinkle seasoning salt or a store-bought BBQ dry rub on the pork. I don't bother to drain the fat from the meat immediately after cooking, but when I store leftovers in the refrigerator, I spoon off any chilled fat that hardens at the top of the container before reheating.

SMART tip: You can also use this marinade for chicken or flank steak. If you don't have a grill, cook the pork in a hot cast-iron skillet or grill pan on the stove, searing all sides to get a nice crust.

Honey-Hoisin Pork Tenderloin

Serves 4

- 2 green onions, (white and green parts), sliced
- ¼ cup hoisin sauce
- ¼ cup low-sodium soy sauce, tamari or coconut aminos
- ¼ cup honey
- 2 tablespoons water
- 3 garlic cloves, minced
- ¼ teaspoon kosher salt
- 1 (1-pound) pork tenderloin, trimmed
- Avocado oil, for the grill
- Steamed sushi or jasmine rice, for serving
- **Garnish:** ½ teaspoon sesame seeds; thinly sliced green onions

In a small bowl, combine the sliced green onions, hoisin, soy sauce, honey, water and garlic. Pour half the marinade into a large plastic bag. Cover and refrigerate the bowl with the remaining marinade.

Salt the pork, add to the bag and seal. Marinate for at least 30 minutes at room temperature or overnight in the refrigerator, turning the bag occasionally.

Preheat the grill to medium-high. Once it's hot, brush down and oil the grates. (It's much easier to clean the grill grates once they've heated and any residual "stuff" has charred. To oil the grill, use avocado oil on a paper towel or old kitchen towel and quickly wipe down the grates.)

Remove pork from the bag and use a paper towel to pat it dry; discard the marinade from the bag. Grill the pork for 15 to 20 minutes, rotating every couple of minutes to sear all sides, until an instant-read thermometer registers 145 degrees. Don't worry if the interior is a little pink as long as you've checked the temperature. Transfer the meat to a cutting board and let it rest for 5 minutes, tented with foil to keep warm. Meanwhile, warm the reserved marinade in the microwave for 30 to 40 seconds or in a small pot on the stove.

Slice the meat and arrange it on a large plate or platter. Drizzle it with the warm marinade and sprinkle with the sesame seeds and thinly sliced green onions. Serve with rice.

notes

This can be cooked in a 450-degree oven for about 15 to 20 minutes, or until the pork registers 145 degrees using an instant-read thermometer.

SMART tip: Using bone-in pork shoulder adds more flavor to the finished carnitas; when the bone easily pulls from the meat, you know it's ready to shred.

Slow Cooker Carnitas Tacos

Serves 6 to 8

2 pounds pork shoulder (preferably bone-in)

2½ teaspoons kosher salt

Freshly ground black pepper

1 tablespoon avocado oil

1 white, yellow or red onion, halved and thinly sliced into half-moons

1 bay leaf

Taco Fixings: Tortillas of choice, warmed; Quick-Pickled Red Onions (page 36); salsa verde or green hot sauce; pico de gallo; avocado slices or guacamole; chopped fresh cilantro; jalapeño slices; or your favorite taco toppings

Dry the pork with paper towels and salt and pepper it all over. In a large sauté pan over medium-high heat, heat the oil. Add the pork and sear it, rotating it to sear all sides, until a crust forms, about 4 minutes per side; be sure to sear the ends as well. (To do this, it's easiest to hold the pork with tongs to keep it in place.)

Transfer the pork to a slow cooker and top it with the onion and bay leaf. Cover and cook on *Low* for about 6 hours.

After 6 hours, shred the pork with two forks. Remove and discard the bone and return the shredded pork to the slow cooker. Change the temperature setting to *Warm* until you're ready to serve. If the meat doesn't fall apart, return it to the slow cooker and set on *High* for an additional 45 to 60 minutes before trying again.

If you'd like to crisp up the pork after it's shredded, spread it in a single layer on a sheet pan and place under a preheated broiler until the edges get caramelized and crispy.

Serve with taco fixings of choice.

notes

I promise there's no need for liquid in this recipe, but I have to mention that because everyone asks. I don't bother to drain the fat from the meat immediately after cooking, but when I store leftovers in the refrigerator, I spoon off any chilled fat that hardens at the top of the container before reheating. If you don't have an onion, you can make it without, and it still turns out delicious.

 **SMART tip** You can find tomato paste in glass jars or in tubes, which can be stored in the refrigerator. That way, you won't end up with a can of tomato paste with just a tablespoon scooped out.

Quick Lamb Ragu

Serves 4

- 1 tablespoon extra virgin olive oil
- ½ yellow, red or white onion, chopped
- 1 carrot, diced (no need to peel)
- 1 celery stalk, diced
- 1 pound ground lamb
- ½ teaspoon kosher salt
- Freshly ground black pepper
- 1 tablespoon tomato paste
- 1 teaspoon fresh thyme leaves, minced
- ½ cup red wine (such as pinot noir or merlot)
- 1 (28-ounce) can tomatoes (whole peeled, diced or crushed)
- ¼ cup water (optional)
- Freshly grated Parmigiano-Reggiano cheese, for serving

In a large skillet over medium heat, heat the olive oil until it shimmers. Add the onions, carrots and celery and cook until the vegetables soften, about 3 minutes. Add the lamb and cook, breaking up the meat with a wooden spoon, until the meat loses its raw red color. Sprinkle the meat and vegetables with salt and pepper. Add the tomato paste, thyme and wine and stir to combine. Bring to a simmer and cook for about 3-4 minutes until the wine reduces, keeping the heat at medium or medium-low.

If you're using whole tomatoes, cut them up with kitchen scissors or break them up with the back of a spoon. Add the tomatoes to the skillet and stir to combine. Simmer on low heat, covered, for 30 minutes to let the flavors come together. Check the sauce; if it starts to brown around the edges of the pan or looks dry, add a couple tablespoons of water to the browned spot and stir. Taste the sauce for salt and adjust if necessary.

Serve over your favorite pasta, spaghetti squash or Creamy Hands-Off Polenta (page 166).

notes

Yes, you can make this with ground beef or ground turkey instead of lamb and I definitely have, but give lamb a chance! It's really delicious.

SMART tip These make a great two-bite appetizer for a dinner party.

Rosemary-Garlic Grilled Lamb Chops

Serves 6

6 garlic cloves, roughly chopped
¼ cup chopped fresh rosemary leaves
1½ teaspoons ground cumin
⅓ cup extra virgin olive oil
Juice of 2 lemons (about ¼ cup)
Freshly ground black pepper
1 teaspoon kosher salt
14 to 16 lamb rib chops (about 4 pounds), frenched and trimmed
Avocado oil, for the grill

In a mini prep food processor, combine the garlic, rosemary, cumin, olive oil, lemon juice, pepper and salt. Lay the lamb chops in a shallow baking dish and pour the marinade over them, turning the meat to coat it well. Marinate the lamb for at least 30 minutes at room temperature or cover and refrigerate overnight. If the chops were in the refrigerator, let sit at room temperature for 20 to 30 minutes before cooking.

Preheat the grill to high. Once it's hot, brush down and oil the grates. (It's much easier to clean the grill grates once they've heated and any residual "stuff" has charred. To oil the grill, use avocado oil on a paper towel or old kitchen towel and quickly wipe down the grates.)

Remove the chops from the marinade and blot them dry with paper towels (otherwise the flames will flare up and char the chops). Discard the marinade. Grill the chops for 3 minutes per side until the internal temperature reaches 145 degrees. If you prefer medium-rare, check the temperature after you flip the chops and pull them off when they reach 135 degrees.

Serve with Crispy Smashed Potatoes (page 160) and Broccolini with Lemon Vinaigrette (page 146).

notes

Lamb is often served with mint jelly, but I think these chops are especially good with a dollop of Chermoula (page 95). You can ask the butcher to french and trim the chops for you. You can use a bullet or small individual smoothie maker for this marinade, but a regular-size food processor will be too big.

SMART tip — Tri-tip is a triangular shape and comes from the very tip of the sirloin. Ask the butcher to remove the silverskin and trim the roast. The black bean sauce I've been using is Lee Kum Kee Black Bean Garlic Sauce, but any Asian black bean sauce or paste will work. It's made from fermented soybeans, not the black beans you may be visualizing.

Grilled Tri-Tip with Black Bean Sauce

Serves 6

1 tri-tip roast (about 2 pounds)
1 tablespoon garlic powder
2½ teaspoons kosher salt
Freshly ground black pepper
¼ cup fermented black bean sauce or black bean garlic sauce
Avocado oil, for the grill

Trim off any silverskin on the meat. Score the meat in a wide crosshatch pattern on both sides. To do this, drag the tip of your knife lightly across the meat, no deeper than a ¼ of an inch, in parallel lines about an inch apart. Then repeat from the other direction to make a diamond pattern. Then flip the meat to score the other side. This helps to tenderize the meat and all those little cuts help the marinade and flavor absorb.

Sprinkle the garlic powder, salt and pepper evenly over the meat and gently rub it in. Spread the black bean paste on the meat, covering the entire surface.

Let the meat sit at room temperature while you preheat the grill to high. Once it's hot, brush down and oil the grates. (It's much easier to clean the grill grates once they've heated and any residual "stuff" has charred. To oil the grill, use avocado oil on a paper towel or old kitchen towel and quickly wipe down the grates.)

Reduce the grill heat to medium-high. Grill the tri-tip for 8 minutes per side, turning once, for medium, which will be an internal temperature of 145 degrees. (Do not poke or move the meat or otherwise mess with it while it's on the grill so you don't lose tasty juices.)

When you remove the meat from the grill, let it rest on a cutting board tented with foil for about 5 minutes before thinly slicing against the grain.

Serve with steamed sushi rice, broccoli or bok choy.

notes

Years ago, my husband begged me not to share this recipe on my blog because it's like a secret weapon we pull out for dinner parties. The credit for its inception goes to our friend Lou Montalvo, who is half Korean and half Puerto Rican and is a great cook. Use flank steak if you can't find tri-tip and score it in the same way. Or use a pork tenderloin and halve the seasonings and black bean paste.

SMART tip Every grill cooks differently, depending on the brand and whether it's a charcoal or gas grill. It's best to use an instant-read meat thermometer when grilling. To take the meat's temperature, insert the probe at an angle into the middle of the thickest part of the meat.

Chile and Espresso–Rubbed Flank Steak

Serves 6

- 1 flank steak (about 2 pounds)
- 1 teaspoon instant espresso powder
- 2 teaspoons ground chile
- 1 teaspoon paprika
- ½ teaspoon garlic powder
- ½ teaspoon ground coriander
- ½ teaspoon ground cumin
- 1 teaspoon kosher salt
- Freshly ground black pepper
- Avocado oil, for the grill
- **Garnish:** Avocado, chopped; sliced green onions; pickled or fresh jalapeño, chopped; fresh cilantro leaves; lime wedges

Score the meat in a wide crosshatch pattern on both sides. To do this, drag the tip of your knife lightly across the meat, no deeper than a ¼ of an inch, in parallel lines about an inch apart. Then repeat from the other direction to make a diamond pattern. Then flip the meat to score the other side. This helps to tenderize the meat and all those little cuts help the marinade and flavor absorb.

In a small bowl, mix the instant espresso, ground chile, paprika, garlic powder, coriander, cumin, salt and pepper. Sprinkle the spice rub on both sides of the flank steak. Marinate at room temperature for at least 30 minutes or cover and refrigerate overnight.

If the meat was in the refrigerator, let it sit at room temperature for 20 to 30 minutes while you preheat the grill to medium-high. Once it's hot, brush down and oil the grates. (It's much easier to clean the grill grates once they've heated and any residual "stuff" has charred. To oil the grill, use avocado oil on a paper towel or old kitchen towel and quickly wipe down the grates.)

Grill the steak, turning once, about 6-8 minutes per side for medium (remove when the internal temperature reaches 145 degrees). For medium-rare, pull the steak off when it reaches 130 to 140 degrees.

Transfer the steak to a cutting board. Let it rest for 5 minutes before thinly slicing against the grain.

Delicious served with Chermoula (page 95), Bread-Free Romesco (page 179) or Avocado-Jalapeño Green Goddess Dip (page 176).

notes

I prefer to use single varietal chile powder such as ancho or arbol, but a chili powder blend works, too. I use Via Roma Espresso Instant Coffee for this recipe, which works better than instant freeze-dried coffee.

SMART tip: Chuck roast might also be labeled as pot roast, a chuck eye roast or a shoulder roast. It's a tough cut of meat that's perfect for slow cooking.

Slow Cooker French Dip Sandwiches

Serves 4 to 6

1 boneless chuck roast (2 to 3 pounds), trimmed of excess fat
½ teaspoon kosher salt
Freshly ground black pepper
2 cups beef stock
2½ tablespoons dried onion soup mix
4 to 6 hoagie or ciabatta rolls, split
4 to 6 slices provolone cheese

Pat the meat dry with a paper towel and sprinkle it with salt and pepper. In the slow cooker, mix the stock and onion soup mix. Add the meat. Cover and cook on *High* for 6 hours or on *Low* for 8 hours, until meat easily shreds.

Transfer the meat to a cutting board and use two forks to pull it apart into large shreds. Ladle the liquid from the slow cooker into individual bowls to use as au jus.

Preheat the broiler. On a half sheet pan, lay out the rolls cut side up; place half a slice of cheese on each side of each roll. Toast briefly under the broiler until the bread is golden and the cheese is melted. Serve the meat on the toasted rolls with au jus on the side for dipping. I add raw carrot and celery sticks for a super easy weeknight meal.

Store leftover meat in the refrigerator for up to 4 days; if any fat accumulates once the meat cools, scrape it off with a spoon.

notes

If you don't have beef stock, use chicken stock or water. I usually sear meat before slow cooking because it creates a nice texture in the finished product. I don't bother here because I'm usually throwing this in the slow cooker in the morning, when our house is busy, so it will be ready in time for dinner.

Soups + Stews

I can eat soup even in the heat of a Texas summer. I love it "all the ways" and could have done an entire cookbook on soups.

Soup is a great thing to make on a Sunday; then you can heat up leftovers for lunch all week long. It's typically very healthy, and a big pot of soup is a great way to use up vegetables that are languishing in your fridge. Most soups freeze like a dream, so go ahead and make a full or double recipe and freeze serving sizes that work for you. I use plastic quart containers or glass containers with tight-fitting lids. I also love Souper Cubes, which are available online—they're like giant silicone ice cube trays, perfect for portioning. Just leave some extra space at the top of the container because liquid will expand as it freezes. Label what you freeze—take it from me, even when you think you will remember, you won't! And use it up within three months for the best flavor possible.

It's easier than you think to make your own stock. For chicken stock, save the bones from a rotisserie chicken or the spine of a spatchcocked chicken. Freeze the bones until you're ready to use! The easiest way for me to make chicken stock is to add the bones (or inexpensive bone-in wings) to the base of my Instant Pot and add carrots, celery, onion or leek and water. Other optional flavor enhancers include peppercorns, a few smashed garlic cloves, a few slices of fresh ginger or a bouquet garni of parsley, bay leaf and thyme. Add a tablespoon of apple cider vinegar to the mix to help extract collagen from the bones. Cook the stock in your Instant Pot for 45 minutes on *High* pressure before straining, cooling and storing for use. In a slow cooker, combine water with chicken bones and aromatics and herbs. Cook on low heat, covered, for 20 to 24 hours or on high heat for 12 to 14 hours; skim any foam that rises to the surface before cooling and storing.

126
Smoky Tomato-Bread Soup

128
Mimi's Baked Potato Soup

130
Green Gazpacho

132
Spring Minestrone

134
Seasonal Minestrone Variations

136
Rotisserie Chicken and Wild Rice Soup

138
Harissa Beef Stew

140
Ramen Made Right

SMART tip: Pimentón de la Vera is smoked paprika from Spain. If you can't find it, use regular paprika or sweet paprika with the addition of ½ teaspoon ground cumin.

Smoky Tomato-Bread Soup

Serves 4 to 6

- ¼ cup extra virgin olive oil
- 1 medium yellow onion, diced (about 1¼ cups)
- ½ teaspoon kosher salt
- 3 garlic cloves, minced
- 2 carrots, diced (no need to peel)
- 2 celery stalks, diced
- 1 (28-ounce) can fire-roasted tomatoes with juice
- 1 teaspoon Pimentón de la Vera or smoked paprika
- 1 (2-inch) slice crusty or rustic sourdough bread (crust on), diced
- 2 cups chicken stock or water
- 8 fresh basil leaves

Garnish: Additional thinly sliced basil leaves; coarse salt; extra virgin olive oil

Instant Pot Directions: Heat the olive oil on the *Sauté* setting and add the onion and kosher salt; cook for 2 minutes, until softened. Add the garlic, carrots and celery. Give the vegetables a stir, then add the tomatoes, pimentón, bread and chicken stock. Close the lid, seal the vent and cook on *Soup* for 10 minutes. When the time is up, use a towel to cover the vent; turn it with tongs to release the steam. (Be very careful not to burn yourself.) Remove the lid and add the basil.

Stovetop Directions: In a large soup pot over medium heat, heat the olive oil. Add the onions and cook 5 to 6 minutes, until softened and slightly golden. Add the garlic, carrots, celery and kosher salt and stir. Cook the vegetables, stirring occasionally, until softened and slightly caramelized, about 5 minutes. Add the tomatoes, pimentón, bread and chicken stock. Cover and simmer on low heat for 20 minutes so the flavors come together, stirring occasionally. Remove the lid and add the basil.

Use an immersion blender to puree the soup, or carefully transfer it in batches to a high-powered blender and puree. To protect yourself from steam, put a kitchen towel on top of the blender lid. Ladle the soup into bowls and top with extra basil, course salt and a drizzle of extra virgin olive oil.

notes

I like to use fire-roasted tomatoes for a touch of smoky flavor, but regular canned tomatoes work well, too. The better the bread you use, the better the soup. I love using a crusty slice from a rustic sourdough loaf. If fresh basil isn't available, don't use dried basil. Use a teaspoon of fresh thyme leaves in the soup and garnish with additional fresh thyme.

SMART tip: Don't overblend this soup or it will turn starchy and slightly gummy. Puree until just combined, and don't be afraid to leave some texture from small chunks of potatoes.

Mimi's Baked Potato Soup

Serves 6

- 2 tablespoons unsalted butter or extra virgin olive oil
- 1 tablespoon all-purpose flour
- 1 teaspoon kosher salt
- 4 cups chicken stock
- 2 leeks (white and light green parts), sliced
- ½ yellow onion, chopped
- 3 medium-large russet potatoes (about 2 pounds total), peeled and cubed
- Tabasco or Crystal hot sauce
- ½ cup milk (skim, 2% or whole)
- Freshly ground black pepper
- **Toppings:** Fresh thyme or chives, chopped; thinly sliced green onion; chopped crunchy bacon; grated sharp cheddar cheese; toasted sourdough croutons

In a medium soup pot over low heat, melt the butter. Whisk in the flour and salt. Whisk in the chicken stock. Add the leeks, onions and potatoes. Bring to a low boil. Cover and cook on low heat for 20 to 25 minutes, until the potatoes are soft.

Add a dash or two of Tabasco. Use an immersion blender to blend the soup in the pot until just smooth, or carefully transfer in batches to a high-powered blender and puree. Taste for salt and pepper and adjust the seasoning if necessary.

Bring the soup back to a low simmer and cook uncovered for about 5 minutes, until it's warm. Stir in the milk and heat for 2 to 3 minutes. Ladle into soup bowls and serve with your choice of garnish.

notes

My Mimi, my mom's mom, made this soup with homemade dumplings floating in the creamy soup. I've omitted those in the interest of carb unloading. If you'd like to make this dairy-free and gluten-free, omit the butter and flour and cook the leek and onion until soft in about a tablespoon of extra virgin olive oil. Add the chicken stock and remaining ingredients and proceed with the recipe. If you don't have leeks, you can use 1 yellow onion.

 **SMART tip** Persian cucumbers are small and have fewer seeds and a tender skin that you don't need to peel. I also love them cut in quarters for dips and crudités trays.

Green Gazpacho

Serves 4 to 6

- 4 small Persian cucumbers, sliced (no need to peel; reserve a few slices for garnish)
- 1 avocado, pitted and peeled
- 3 or 4 small yellow tomatoes, quartered, with their juice, or 1½ cups yellow cherry tomatoes
- 3 green onions (white and green parts), sliced
- 1 garlic clove, smashed and peeled
- ½ cup packed fresh cilantro leaves and stems
- ¼ cup sherry vinegar
- ¼ cup extra virgin olive oil
- ½ cup hulled raw pumpkin seeds (pepitas), sunflower seeds, or sliced or slivered almonds
- ½ serrano or jalapeño chile, seeded
- 1 teaspoon honey or light agave nectar
- Juice of 1 lemon
- ½ teaspoon kosher salt
- Freshly ground black pepper
- **Garnish:** Extra virgin olive oil; coarse salt; the reserved cucumber slices; additional pepitas or sunflower seeds; fresh cilantro leaves

In a high-powered blender, combine the cucumbers, avocado, tomatoes, green onions, garlic, cilantro, vinegar, olive oil, pepitas, chile, honey, lemon juice, kosher salt and pepper. Blend until smooth. Taste and adjust the flavor as preferred with more acidity, more jalapeño or more salt. Depending on the sweetness of the tomatoes, add more honey to sweeten if you like. Chill before serving.

Garnish the soup with a drizzle of olive oil, a sprinkle of coarse salt, the reserved cucumber, and more pepitas or cilantro leaves if you like.

notes

You can make this a day or two ahead without the avocado; just add the avocado and puree again just before serving. I prefer to chill the soup for at least 30 minutes to an hour, but it's also good at room temperature. You can use a large regular or English cucumber to replace the Persian cucumbers; just be sure to peel. If yellow tomatoes aren't in season or you can't find them, don't sub red ones; they will turn the gazpacho brown.

SMART tip: Save parmesan rinds for brothy soups and tomato sauces for extra flavors. I add one to soup when I add the stock, then remove it before serving. It gives an extra layer of rich flavor and umami.

Spring Minestrone

Serves 4 to 6

- 2 tablespoons extra virgin olive oil
- 2 leeks (white and light green parts), chopped
- Kosher salt
- 2 celery stalks, sliced
- 2 carrots, sliced (no need to peel)
- 6 ounces sugar snap peas, trimmed, sliced in half crosswise (about 1½ cups)
- 1 cup packed roughly chopped greens (spinach, arugula, kale or Swiss chard leaves)
- 1 cup shelled fresh peas
- ½ bunch asparagus, woody parts trimmed, sliced into 1-inch pieces
- ½ teaspoon kosher salt
- ⅛ teaspoon ground white pepper or freshly ground black pepper
- 4 cups chicken or vegetable stock or water
- 1 (15-ounce) can cannellini or navy beans, drained and rinsed
- 1 teaspoon minced fresh thyme leaves
- Parmigiano-Reggiano cheese rind (optional)
- **Garnish:** Shaved Parmigiano-Reggiano; extra virgin olive oil; coarse salt

In a medium Dutch oven or soup pot, heat the olive oil. Add the leeks and a pinch of salt and cook until soft, about 2 minutes. Add the celery, carrots, sugar snap peas, greens, peas, asparagus, ½ teaspoon kosher salt and the pepper. Stir to combine. Add the chicken stock, beans, thyme and parmesan rind, if using. Cover and cook on medium heat for 20 minutes, or until the vegetables soften.

Remove the parmesan rind. Taste for seasoning. Serve, garnished with shaved parmesan, a drizzle of olive oil and a sprinkle of salt.

notes

Feel free to swap a chopped onion for the leeks. To keep vegan, use vegetable stock or water and omit the parmesan rind.

Seasonal Minestrone Variations

Depending on what's in season, substitute the vegetables in the Spring version with what you have on hand. Almost any leafy green can be used. And when asparagus and sugar snap peas aren't in season, turn to what's fresh. Here's an outline of what you can use at various times of the year.

Summer Minestrone

1 chopped zucchini

1 cup chopped fresh spinach

1 cup chopped fresh tomatoes

6 ounces fresh green beans, trimmed and cut in thirds

Fall Minestrone

1½ cups cubed butternut squash

½ pound small red potatoes, chopped (about 6 potatoes)

1 cup chopped Swiss chard, stems thinly sliced

6 ounces fresh green beans, trimmed and cut in thirds

Winter Minestrone

1 medium sweet potato, peeled and cubed

4 or 5 kale leaves, center stem removed, chopped

1 cup thinly sliced cabbage

notes

All the variations of this soup freeze well, so don't be afraid of leftovers!

SMART tip You can make this with cooked brown or white rice instead of wild rice; just stir in a cup of cooked rice and let it warm with the soup before serving.

Rotisserie Chicken and Wild Rice Soup (Instant Pot or Slow Cooker)

Serves 4 to 6

- 2 tablespoons extra virgin olive oil
- ½ red, white or yellow onion, chopped
- 1 leek (white and light green parts), chopped
- 2 garlic cloves, minced
- 2 celery stalks, chopped
- 8 ounces cremini or button mushrooms, sliced
- 10 fresh thyme sprigs and 1 bay leaf, tied together with butcher twine
- 1 teaspoon kosher salt
- 4 cups chicken stock
- 2 cups shredded rotisserie chicken
- 1 cup uncooked wild rice
- 1 cup half-and-half

Garnish: ¼ cup minced fresh flat-leaf parsley; coarse salt

Instant Pot Directions: Heat the olive oil on the *Sauté* setting and add the onion. Stir and cook until softened, about 2 minutes. Add the leek, garlic, celery, mushrooms, thyme, bay leaf, kosher salt and chicken stock and stir. Close the lid, seal the vent and cook on *Soup* or *Manual* for 15 minutes. When the time is up, use a towel to cover the vent; turn it with tongs to release the steam. (Be very careful not to burn yourself.) Open the lid and stir in the chicken and wild rice. Seal the lid and valve again and set to *Soup* or *Manual* for 15 additional minutes. Once it finishes, carefully release the pressure manually and remove the lid. Remove the thyme and bay leaf and discard. Stir in the half-and-half.

Stovetop Directions: In a 4-quart soup pot over medium heat, heat the olive oil. Add the onions and stir until softened, about 2 minutes. Add leeks, garlic, celery, mushrooms, thyme, bay leaf, kosher salt and chicken stock and stir. Bring to a low boil, reduce heat to medium-low, cover and cook for 15 minutes. Add the shredded chicken and wild rice and stir. Cover again and continue to cook for another 20 minutes, until wild rice softens but still has a little crunch.

Remove the thyme and bay leaf and discard. In the stovetop version, some of the liquid will evaporate from the pot. If the soup looks dry, add another cup or two of stock or water and another pinch of kosher salt. Stir in the half-and-half.

Ladle into soup bowls and top with parsley and coarse salt.

notes

This is a great soup to make for someone who's not feeling well because the flavors are comforting and not too heavy. I make this in the Instant Pot when I need to prepare dinner in the early afternoon because of a crazy after-school schedule. You can leave it plugged in on *Keep Warm* and it will be ready to serve when you walk in the door.

SMART tip It's important that the pieces of meat don't touch each other while browning; otherwise, they will steam instead of sear.

Harissa Beef Stew

Serves 6 to 8

- 2 tablespoons extra virgin olive oil
- 3 pounds beef stew meat, cut in 2-inch cubes
- ½ teaspoon kosher salt
- Freshly ground black pepper
- 4 garlic cloves, minced
- 1 yellow, red or white onion, chopped
- 1½ or 2½ cups beef or chicken stock
- 1 tablespoon balsamic vinegar
- 3 tablespoons tomato paste
- 2 teaspoons harissa paste
- ½ teaspoon smoked or regular paprika
- 3 carrots, sliced (no need to peel)
- 8 small Yukon gold or red potatoes, quartered
- 2 tablespoons arrowroot powder or corn starch (optional)

Garnish: Minced fresh flat-leaf parsley; coarse salt

Instant Pot Directions: Heat the olive oil on the *Sauté* setting and sear the meat in batches, being careful not to overcrowd the pan. Add a sprinkle of kosher salt and pepper as it browns. Return the browned meat and the juices to the pot and add garlic, onions, 1½ cups stock, the vinegar, tomato paste, harissa, paprika and more salt and pepper. Select the *Manual/High* pressure setting and set it to 40 minutes, making sure the vent is sealed. When the time is up, use a towel to cover the vent and turn it with tongs to release the steam. (Be very careful not to burn yourself.) Open the lid, add the carrots and potatoes and stir. Close the lid, seal the valve and set again to *Manual/High* pressure for 5 minutes. After the vegetables cook, carefully release the steam again and open the lid. If the stew seems too thin, remove a cup of cooking liquid and whisk in arrowroot. Add the mixture back to the pot and stir. Set the pot to the *Sauté* setting and cook uncovered for 10 minutes, stirring until thickened.

Stovetop Directions: Heat the oil in a large Dutch oven or stockpot over medium heat and sear the meat in batches, adding salt and pepper as it cooks. Transfer the meat from the pot to a plate and set aside. Over medium heat, add the garlic and onions to the same pot and cook until softened, 2 to 3 minutes. Add 2½ cups beef stock, the vinegar, tomato paste, harissa, paprika, carrots, potatoes, salt and a few grindings of fresh pepper. Return the meat and its juices to the pot, cover and simmer on low heat until the meat is very tender, 2 to 3½ hours. If the liquid level gets too low, add more stock or water as needed. The meat should be very tender; if it's tough, let it continue to simmer, covered, for an additional 20 minutes. If the stew is too thin, remove a cup of cooking liquid from the pot and whisk in the arrowroot. Add the mixture back to the pot and stir. Simmer uncovered for 10 minutes until the stew is thick.

Taste the stew for seasoning, garnish with parsley and coarse salt and serve.

 **SMART tip** If you don't feel like cooking a soft-boiled egg, whisk an egg in a small bowl and slowly add it to the hot soup while stirring in a circular motion. You'll end up with a richly flavored egg drop soup.

Ramen Made Right

Serves 4 to 6

1 package instant ramen (vegetable, chicken or beef flavor)

Optional Additions

¼ cup chopped fresh leafy greens (such as spinach or bok choy)

½ cup cubed silken tofu, in ½-inch pieces

1 tablespoon mellow white miso or yellow miso

1 teaspoon sriracha, chili oil or chili paste

1 tablespoon chopped kimchi

1 teaspoon toasted or regular sesame oil

1 teaspoon low-sodium soy sauce, tamari or coconut aminos

1 nori sheet, roughly torn into pieces

1 teaspoon furikake

1 or 2 green onions (white and green parts), thinly sliced

¼ cup bean sprouts

¼ cup sliced fresh mushrooms

1 tablespoon chopped fresh herbs (such as cilantro, basil or mint)

1 soft-boiled egg

Make the ramen according to package directions. If you're using the greens, add them while the noodles simmer. When you add the flavoring packet, add any of the other suggested additions for bulk and flavor. (My favorites are a little chili oil, sesame oil, sliced green onions and a soft-boiled egg.) If adding the egg, place it on top of the noodles just before serving.

notes

Furikake is a Japanese seasoning made with flaked seaweed, sesame seeds and dried fish. It's delicious sprinkled on steamed rice, roasted broccoli or salmon. The ramen I buy is Nongshim Shin Gourmet Spicy Ramyun; it comes with an extra spice packet that adds great flavor. But you can also make this with Maruchan Ramen, available at most grocery stores.

Sides

Keep it simple. Roast almost any seasonal vegetable with olive oil, lemon, crushed red pepper flakes and salt.

Or chop up a hodgepodge of leafy greens and wilt them in a pan with olive oil, garlic, maybe a little anchovy paste and lemon. One of my favorite combinations is Swiss chard, arugula, spinach and kale, all of which I grow in my garden. Since I am no expert on gardening, my philosophy is: If I can do it, you can do it.

If you have younger kids who aren't adventurous, I suggest always giving them a type of vegetable they like and will eat as well as something new off your plate that has more flavor. You can broaden their palate while still (hopefully) getting some veggies in them.

Don't get hung up on which veggie sides to pair with a main dish. Use what's in season, what sounds good or what happens to be in your fridge. Remember the mantra of this book: Don't stress!

146 Broccolini with Lemon Vinaigrette

148 Pan-Roasted Shishito Peppers

150 Oven-Roasted Mini Sweet Peppers

152 Za'atar Green Beans

154 Soy-Sesame Spinach

156 Roasted Zucchini with Marcona Almond–Rosemary Crunch

158 Balsamic Brussels Sprouts and Butternut Squash

160 Crispy Smashed Potatoes

162 Honey-Harissa Roasted Root Vegetables

164 Sweet Potatoes with Brown Sugar Glaze

166 Creamy Hands-Off Polenta

SMART tip: Half my family prefers Broccolini and broccoli roasted, and the other half likes them simmered or steamed within an inch of their life. I've come to appreciate both versions. Use 1 large head of broccoli instead of Broccolini if you prefer. Cut it into small florets and slice the stalks into thin coins.

Broccolini with Lemon Vinaigrette

Serves 4 to 6

---

2 to 4 tablespoons extra virgin olive oil

½ teaspoon crushed red pepper flakes

2 tablespoons fresh lemon juice

½ teaspoon kosher salt, divided

Freshly ground black pepper

1 teaspoon anchovy paste or 1 anchovy fillet, finely chopped (optional)

3 bunches Broccolini (about 1½ pounds)

Lemon vinaigrette: In a small bowl, combine 2 tablespoons of the olive oil, red pepper flakes, lemon juice, ¼ teaspoon of the salt and the pepper. Add the anchovy, if you like. (I love adding it here, but you do you. I promise it won't taste "fishy.") Whisk until combined. Set aside.

Trim the stem ends of the Broccolini. Cut any thicker pieces in half lengthwise.

Roasting Directions: Preheat the oven to 425 degrees; use the convection roast setting if you have it. Line a half sheet pan with parchment paper. Place the Broccolini in a pile on the sheet pan and drizzle with 2 tablespoons olive oil. Toss to coat, then spread it out in a single layer. Sprinkle with the remaining salt. Roast for 30 to 35 minutes, until slightly crispy and golden.

Steaming Directions: In a medium saucepan over high heat, add 1 cup water and bring to a simmer. Add the Broccolini along with a sprinkle of salt and a teaspoon of olive oil. Turn the heat to low, cover and simmer for about 15-20 minutes or until soft and a fork easily punctures the stems. Transfer the Broccolini with a slotted spoon or tongs and paper towels to drain.

Arrange the cooked Broccolini on a platter or individual plates, drizzle with the vinaigrette and serve.

notes

When steaming the Broccolini, I sometimes add a pinch of crushed red pepper flakes to the water to help spice up the simmering liquid. You could also add the rind of the lemon that was used for the vinaigrette. I often add those lemon rinds to the sheet pan when roasting—it softens them so they will yield an extra squeeze of juice at the end. The lemon vinaigrette is also delicious over roasted or steamed cauliflower. Fun fact: Sometimes called baby broccoli, Broccolini is a hybrid of broccoli and Chinese broccoli (kai-lan) was trademarked in 1993 by Japan's Sakata Seed Corporation.

SMART tip — Shishito peppers are a form of Russian roulette; be aware that one in ten is super spicy. When we eat them at home, we're always staring at each other to figure out who gets a spicy one.

Pan-Roasted Shishito Peppers

Serves 2 to 4

2 tablespoons extra virgin olive oil

6 ounces shishito peppers (about 25 peppers)

½ lemon

½ teaspoon coarse salt

Dipping sauce (optional): Spicy Rémoulade (page 94) or Homemade Buttermilk Ranch Dressing (page 38)

In a cast-iron skillet or wide sauté pan over medium-high heat, heat the olive oil until it is hot but not smoking. Add the peppers in a single layer. Wait for 2 to 3 minutes before stirring, so the peppers can blister in the hot pan. It will take 8 to 10 minutes to soften and char a pan full of peppers.

Toss the peppers with a squeeze of lemon juice and the salt. Slide the peppers into a bowl or small platter and serve hot with a dipping sauce if you like. You pick them up by the stem end and eat them whole (minus the stem, of course!).

notes

Instead of salt, try topping the shishito peppers with Everything Bagel Seasoning or za'atar — delicious!

 **SMART tip** It may seem like a lot of olive oil, and you can cut it in half if you like, but it's so delicious soaked up with crusty bread. You can store remaining oil in the refrigerator to use for frittatas or pasta dishes.

Oven-Roasted Mini Sweet Peppers

Serves 4 to 6

1 pound tri-color mini peppers, kept whole with stems on
¼ cup extra virgin olive oil
½ teaspoon kosher salt
4 fresh thyme sprigs

Preheat the oven to 350 degrees.

In a small ceramic or glass baking dish, combine the peppers, olive oil and salt. Add the thyme sprigs and push them into the olive oil. Roast for 45 minutes or until peppers are browned in spots, slightly wrinkled and softened.

Serve these peppers on top of crostini with Simple Whipped Feta (page 178) or on a cheese board.

 **notes**

These are also delicious with a tablespoon of balsamic vinegar added to the pan before roasting, or drizzled with store-bought balsamic glaze right after they come out of the oven. I use a medium-size oval dish to bake these peppers, but you can also use an 8-inch square baking dish.

> **SMART tip**
> This spice mix can be combined with olive oil as a dip for bread or on roasted chicken, salmon or vegetables. Store in the pantry in a glass container with a tight-fitting lid.

Za'atar Green Beans

Serves 4

1 pound haricots verts or thin green beans, trimmed
1 tablespoon extra virgin olive oil
½ teaspoon kosher salt
Freshly ground black pepper
1 tablespoon Homemade Za'atar (recipe follows)

Preheat the oven to 400 degrees; use the convection roast setting if you have it.

On a parchment paper-lined half sheet pan, add the green beans in a pile. Drizzle with the olive oil and toss to combine. Spread out in a single layer. Sprinkle with the salt and pepper. Roast on the top rack of the oven for 25 to 30 minutes, until golden brown. Sprinkle with the za'atar and serve warm.

Homemade Za'atar
2 tablespoons dried thyme leaves
2 tablespoons white sesame seeds
2 teaspoons ground sumac
½ teaspoon kosher salt

Stir together all the ingredients in a small bowl.

notes

Instead of za'atar, you can use Everything Bagel Seasoning, plain sesame seeds or seasoning salt. If using seasoning salt, cut the kosher salt in half. If you can't find sumac at your grocery store, it's available online. The green beans will get roasted and browned in spots, which makes them crispy and delicious—almost like green bean fries.

 **SMART tip** Make a triple recipe of the soy-sesame mixture and store the extra in the fridge to flavor steamed broccoli, bok choy or sautéed sugar snap peas. Drizzle it on rice or use as a dumpling sauce.

Soy-Sesame Spinach

Serves 4

- 1 tablespoon plus 1 teaspoon low-sodium soy sauce, tamari or coconut aminos
- 1 tablespoon unseasoned rice vinegar
- 2 teaspoons toasted or regular sesame oil
- 2 tablespoons avocado oil
- 6-7 cups packed baby spinach, about 10 ounces
- 1 tablespoon sesame seeds

In a small bowl, mix the soy sauce, vinegar and sesame oil. Set aside.

Heat the avocado oil in a large skillet over medium-high heat. Working in batches, add the spinach, tossing and letting it cook down slightly before adding more, until just wilted, about 2 minutes. Add a couple tablespoons of water if the spinach starts to stick to the pan.

Reduce the heat to medium. Pour the soy sauce mixture over the spinach and stir to combine. Top with the sesame seeds and serve.

notes

If you want to add a little kick, mix ½ teaspoon crushed red pepper flakes or sriracha into the soy sauce mixture. Make this with almost any type of greens, such as Swiss chard or kale.

SMART tip: I always pull rosemary and thyme leaves off their stems backwards.

Roasted Zucchini with Marcona Almond–Rosemary Crunch

Serves 4

3 tablespoons extra virgin olive oil, divided
½ cup Marcona almonds, chopped
¼ cup fresh rosemary leaves, minced
1 garlic clove, minced
½ teaspoon crushed red pepper flakes
1 pound zucchini (about 3 medium), ends trimmed, cut lengthwise into quarters
½ teaspoon kosher salt
Freshly ground black pepper

Move a rack to the top spot in the oven. Preheat the oven to 400 degrees. Line a sheet pan with parchment paper.

In a sauté pan over medium heat, heat 1½ tablespoons of the olive oil until shimmering, about 30 seconds. Add the almonds, rosemary, garlic and red pepper flakes. Stir occasionally for about a minute until it becomes fragrant and the rosemary is slightly browned, being careful not to burn the garlic. Remove from the heat and transfer the mixture to a plate to cool.

Place the zucchini on the prepared sheet pan. Drizzle with remaining 1½ tablespoons olive oil and sprinkle with the salt and black pepper. Roast for 25 to 30 minutes on the top rack until softened and slightly browned at the edges.

Transfer the zucchini to a platter and top with the almond mixture. Serve warm.

notes

Use this same almond topping for other roasted vegetables such as summer squash, asparagus or broccoli florets. If you don't have Marcona almonds, just use regular roasted almonds, chopped pistachios or walnuts.

 **SMART tip** Save leftover veggies to toss into green salads later in the week!

Balsamic Brussels Sprouts and Butternut Squash

Serves 4 to 6

3 tablespoons balsamic vinegar

2 teaspoons honey

¾ teaspoon kosher salt, divided

2 pounds Brussels sprouts

1 small butternut squash, peeled, seeded and cubed (about 2 cups)

½ red onion, cut in ½-inch strips

¼ cup extra virgin olive oil

Coarse salt, to finish

In a small bowl, combine the balsamic vinegar, honey and ¼ teaspoon of the kosher salt. Set aside.

Preheat the oven to 400 degrees. Use the convection roast setting if you have it to help the Brussels caramelize.

Rinse and dry the Brussels sprouts and trim the root ends. Cut them in half from top to bottom, through the base. Discard any yellowed or blemished leaves. If other leaves fall off, keep them to add to the pan; they make tasty chips. Add the sprouts, butternut squash and red onion to a half sheet pan and drizzle with the olive oil. Toss to coat in the oil, then spread out the vegetables in a single layer, with the sprouts cut side down. Top with the remaining ½ teaspoon of kosher salt.

Roast for 40 minutes or until golden brown. Remove from the oven and immediately drizzle with the balsamic mixture while the vegetables are still on the hot pan. (The residual heat from the pan will help the glaze reduce a tiny bit.) Use a spatula to release and gently toss the vegetables. Add a sprinkle of coarse salt and serve.

notes

Use pre-chopped butternut squash to make your prep super fast. To add color, top the roasted vegetables with pomegrante seeds.

SMART tip: Any time you boil potatoes or blanch vegetables in boiling water, if you add a generous amount of kosher salt to the cooking water you'll end up with more flavorful vegetables.

Crispy Smashed Potatoes

Serves 4 to 6

---

1 pound small waxy potatoes such as Yukon golds, about 2 inches in diameter

¼ cup kosher salt (Don't panic! It's for the cooking liquid.)

¼ cup extra virgin olive oil

Freshly ground black pepper

½ cup sour cream or crème fraîche

Garnish: Chopped fresh flat-leaf parsley, dill or chives; coarse salt

---

Preheat the oven to 450 degrees; use the convection roast setting if you have it.

Bring a large pot of water to boil with ¼ cup of the kosher salt. (The salt in the cooking water will enhance the flavor of the potatoes as they cook.) Boil the potatoes until just fork tender, about 15 minutes. (The time will vary depending on the size of the potatoes; be careful not to overcook or they'll fall apart when smashed.) Drain well in a colander, then immediately turn them out onto a kitchen towel and let them dry in a single layer for a few minutes. Transfer the potatoes to a half sheet pan. (You can line the sheet pan with parchment paper first for easier cleanup, but the potatoes will end up crispier if you don't.)

Place another rimmed sheet pan on top and push down firmly to smash the potatoes. (When my youngest was little, I used to let her stand on top of the second sheet pan to smash the potatoes. Don't worry, that pan got moved to the sink afterwards.) You can also use the bottom of a water glass or mug to smash each potato individually. Drizzle a little olive oil over each potato, then move the potatoes around on the pan to make sure they're well coated. Sprinkle with kosher salt and black pepper. Roast the potatoes until crispy and golden brown, 35 to 40 minutes.

Spread the sour cream on a large plate or platter and top with the potatoes. Garnish with fresh herbs and a sprinkle of coarse salt and serve.

notes

Make this without sour cream to keep it dairy-free, but the sour cream makes the crispy potatoes taste like grown-up potato skins. I also use these flattened potatoes as vehicles for nacho toppings or chili and shredded cheese. Or serve drizzled with Chermoula (page 95) or Bread-Free Romesco (page 179).

SMART tip — Cut the veggies into the same size pieces so they cook at the same rate. I've given you a general size of vegetables to look for, but it doesn't make a huge difference so don't stress about the size.

Honey-Harissa Roasted Root Vegetables

Serves 4

- 1 large sweet potato, peeled and chopped
- 1 medium parsnip, peeled, cored and chopped
- 2 large carrots, chopped (no need to peel)
- 1 medium rutabaga, peeled and chopped
- 4 shallots, peeled and quartered
- ¼ cup honey
- 1-2 teaspoons harissa paste
- 2 tablespoons extra virgin olive oil
- 1½ teaspoons kosher salt

Garnish: Fresh rosemary leaves; coarse salt; crushed red pepper flakes

Preheat the oven to 400 degrees. (I don't recommend using convection here because honey can easily burn at high heat.) Line a rimmed half sheet pan with parchment paper.

In a large bowl, combine the sweet potato, parsnip, carrots, rutabaga, shallots, honey, harissa, olive oil and salt and toss to coat. Transfer the vegetables to the prepared pan and spread them in a single layer.

Roast for 45 to 50 minutes, using a spatula to scrape and toss the vegetables halfway through cooking, until the vegetables are tender and beginning to brown. Remove from the oven, sprinkle with rosemary or red pepper flakes and serve immediately.

notes

This easy side dish is just as perfect with a weeknight roast chicken as it is on your Thanksgiving table. Use a 9x13-inch ceramic baking dish if you like, but no need to line with parchment paper. Feel free to use about ½ pound Yukon gold potatoes (the skin can stay on) instead of the sweet potato. If you can't find rutabagas, leave them out or substitute extra parsnips or carrots. Add a couple of peeled and chopped beets to the vegetables for added color, or any other root vegetables or tubers you love, such as turnips or small red potatoes. Harissa is a spicy paste, usually sold in glass jars or tubes. It can be found in your grocery store's international aisle or online.

SMART tip: We typically have this at Thanksgiving, but it's one of those dishes I wish I'd make more often. You could always cut the butter and brown sugar in half for a weeknight version.

Sweet Potatoes with Brown Sugar Glaze

Serves 4 to 6

- 4 or 5 sweet potatoes or garnet yams (about 3 pounds), washed and pricked all over with a fork
- ½ cup unsalted butter, cut into cubes
- 1½ cups packed dark brown sugar
- 2 tablespoons water
- ½ teaspoon kosher salt

If you are baking the sweet potatoes in the oven, preheat to 425 degrees. Line a half sheet pan with parchment paper and add the sweet potatoes. Place on the top rack of the oven and bake for 45 minutes or until a fork can easily be inserted into the potato. Alternatively, cook on a microwave-safe plate according to your microwave's directions. Set aside to cool.

Reduce the oven heat to 375 degrees, or preheat it to 375 degrees if you cooked the sweet potatoes in the microwave.

Once the sweet potatoes are cool enough to handle, use your fingers or a paring knife to tear away the skin. Slice the sweet potatoes into 1-inch rounds and place in a single layer in a ceramic or glass 9x13-inch pan. Depending on the size of your potatoes, you may need two baking pans. Set aside.

In a small saucepan over medium-low heat, melt the butter. Add the brown sugar, water and salt and stir well to combine. Spoon the brown sugar glaze evenly over the top of each sweet potato round. Bake for about 20 minutes, until the brown sugar is melted and the sweet potatoes are glazed. As this bakes in the oven, some of the glaze will melt off the top of the sweet potatoes, onto the pan. Let cool for 5 to 10 minutes (the glaze is very hot) then serve, spooning any melted brown sugar glaze over the top.

notes

Instead of dark brown sugar you can substitute light brown sugar, coconut sugar or muscovado sugar. To turn this into delicious mashed sweet potatoes, use a fork to mix together the topping and potatoes and bake in a 350-degree oven for 15-20 minutes.

 **SMART tip** This hands-off oven method for cooking polenta was adapted from two of my favorite food writers Alexandra Stafford and Paula Wolfert's original recipe.

Creamy Hands-Off Polenta

Serves 4 to 6

1 or 2 tablespoons unsalted butter or olive oil

1 cup medium-coarse or coarse cornmeal or polenta (preferably stone ground, not quick-cooking)

4½ cups or 5 cups water, vegetable stock or chicken stock

1 cup milk (skim, 2% or whole)

Kosher salt and freshly ground black pepper

Garnish: About ½ cup freshly grated Parmigiano-Reggiano cheese

Oven Directions: Preheat the oven to 350 degrees. Grease a large oven-proof baking dish or a Dutch oven with 1 tablespoon butter. Pour in the polenta, water, milk, the remaining butter and 1 teaspoon salt, and stir with a fork or whisk until blended. Don't worry, the mixture won't come together but it will when cooked.

Bake uncovered for 40 minutes, then carefully stir the polenta. Continue to bake uncovered for another 15 to 20 minutes, until mostly set. Remove from the oven. The polenta will still look loose but will thicken as it cools. Taste for seasoning and stir in pepper and more salt if needed.

Instant Pot Directions: Combine 1 tablespoon butter, the polenta, 5 cups water and 1 teaspoon salt in the Instant Pot. The milk is omitted in the Instant Pot version because the milk would scald and the additional liquid isn't needed because it doesn't evaporate from a sealed Instant Pot.

Cook on *Manual/High* pressure with the vent sealed for 10 minutes. Let the pressure release naturally. Remove the cover. Taste for seasoning and stir in pepper and more salt if needed.

Top the polenta with the parmesan and serve. I like to top polenta with Lamb Ragu (page 112), meatballs, Pomodoro Sauce (page 56) or slow-cooked short ribs.

notes

Polenta is coarsely ground cornmeal—basically grits, for all my Southern people. The milk in the oven method can be replaced with stock or water.

Snacks

On vacation or in the summer, I love nothing more than a snack board for dinner. When it's too hot to cook, I pull together some vegetables, cheeses and crackers for dinner and call it a night.

Bring on the crudités, some flavorful dips, nuts, olives and dried fruit! Healthy snacks are a great way to get more vegetables in your kiddos, especially when they come home famished from a day at school or a sports practice. The trick is to have veggies pre-cut and stored in the fridge so they're just as easy to grab as a "snack pack" from the pantry.

Cheese boards have become quite the thing in recent years and they're easy to make at home. I've given you a checklist to create your own. Just pack everything close together and pre-cut hard cheeses so they're easy to nosh on. I also love a chocolate and berry board as an easy "no bake" dessert. Just grab several favorite chocolates, both milk and dark, plus berries and nuts. Delicious!

A story about the deviled eggs at the end of this chapter: During the beginning of the pandemic in 2020, my kids and I would be up reading or watching movies late into the night. One night around midnight, my son and I made a batch of the deviled egg recipe and polished it off ourselves. It was the perfect midnight snack.

172 Snack Board Checklist

176 Avocado-Jalapeño Green Goddess Dip

178 Simple Whipped Feta

179 Bread-Free Romesco

180 White Bean Dip with Rosemary Olive Oil

182 Edamame Hummus

183 Spicy Roasted Garbanzos

184 Cocktail Nuts with Rosemary and Sage

186 Deviled Eggs with Peas and Dill

Snack Board Checklist

For a cheese board, choose 3 to 5 cheeses. Once you develop an arsenal of favorites, there's no need to stray from what's working. Just stick with your tried-and-true cheeses and change up the condiments and extras. I also like to "mess up" the cheeses and cut into them a little, so guests aren't afraid to jump in. Hard cheeses like Gouda and Manchego can be pre-sliced with a sharp knife and fanned out on the board to make them more manageable.

For a crudités board, use a colorful variety of your favorite veggies, along with extras like salty nuts, tangy olives or cornichons, or even slices of baguette or pita. Serve with a couple dips from this chapter, or Homemade Ranch Dressing (see page 38). There's also nothing better to take to a new mom than a cheese and crudités board—when you're holding a baby and have no time to sit for a meal, you can graze to your heart's content.

Serving Pieces
- Wood board (even a wooden cutting board)
- Cheese knives
- Small bowls for dips, olives or cornichons
- Small forks for olives and an extra small bowl for the pits
- Small plates
- Napkins

Veggies for Crudités Board
- Bell pepper slices
- Mini sweet peppers
- Cucumber slices or spears
- Celery sticks
- Blanched asparagus
- Carrot sticks
- Radish slices
- Endive spears
- Cherry tomatoes
- Sugar snap peas
- Broccoli, cauliflower or Romanesco florets
- Jicama slices

Clockwise: Edamame Hummus, Bread-Free Romesco, White Bean Dip with Rosemary Olive Oil, Avocado-Jalapeño Green Goddess Dip, Simple Whipped Feta

Cheeses

The goal is a combination of soft fresh cheeses and firm aged cheeses so you have various textures. I also like to have a mix of cow's milk, sheep's milk and goat's milk cheeses.

Humboldt Fog (goat cheese)
Plain chèvre (goat cheese) log that you can roll in minced fresh herbs and salt
Triple cream Brie, such as St. André (cow's milk)
Mimolette, (aged cow's milk cheese)
Aged Gouda (cow's milk)
Manchego (sheep's milk)
Pecorino, such as Pecorino Romano or one labeled Semi-stagionato, which will be slightly aged and a little salty (sheep's milk)
Stilton or a creamy blue cheese (cow's milk)
Aged white cheddar (cow's milk)

Charcuterie

Prosciutto
Jambon de Bayonne (French cured ham)
Mortadella
Hard salami

Bread

Water crackers
Seeded crackers
Breadsticks
Flatbread
Sliced baguette
Rice crackers, almond crackers or endive spears for gluten-free options

Fruit

Dried cherries
Dried apricots
Blackberries
Figs
Apple slices
Pear slices
Grapes
Candied orange rind
Pomegranate seeds

Nuts

Toasted pecans
Pistachios
Marcona almonds
Cocktail Nuts with Rosemary and Sage (page 184)

Condiments and Extras

Jam (such as fig jam)
Quince paste
Mustards (if serving meats)
Cornichons
Olives
Spicy Roasted Garbanzos (page 183)

Sweets

Dark chocolate, broken up in bite-size chunks
Honey or honeycomb
Chocolate covered almonds
Chocolate covered dried fruits
Candied ginger

Spicy Roasted Garbanzos, Cocktail Nuts with Rosemary and Sage

SMART tip: Serve this tangy dip with raw crudités, grilled vegetables, grilled steak or salmon. Thin the dip with a little water and use it as a salad dressing. You may want a touch more salt if you add water, so taste the dressing before serving.

Avocado-Jalapeño Green Goddess Dip

Makes about 2 cups

- 1½ cups packed fresh cilantro (leaves and stems)
- 1½ cups packed fresh flat-leaf parsley (leaves and stems)
- 3 tablespoons minced fresh chives
- 3 tablespoons minced fresh mint leaves
- 2 green onions (white and green parts), sliced
- 1 avocado, pitted, peeled and chopped
- 1 tablespoon chopped seeded jalapeño chile
- 2 garlic cloves, roughly chopped
- Juice of 1 to 2 limes
- ¾ cup plain Greek yogurt
- ½ cup well-shaken buttermilk
- ¼ teaspoon kosher salt
- Freshly ground black pepper

In a food processor, add all the ingredients. Puree well until the herbs are uniformly chopped and the dip is creamy. Taste for seasoning and adjust if necessary. Store in an airtight container for up to a week.

notes

You can use about 2 tablespoons chopped white onion instead of the green onions. And if you don't have an avocado, I've made this without and it's still delicious.

SMART tip — Feta packed in brine is creamier and doesn't contain the potato starch or cellulose powder usually found in pre-crumbled cheeses.

Simple Whipped Feta

Makes about 2 cups

½ cup plain Greek yogurt (I use 2% but any type will work)
8 ounces good-quality feta cheese (preferably packed in brine, not pre-crumbled)
¼ cup water
3 tablespoons extra virgin olive oil
1 garlic clove, roughly chopped
1 tablespoon fresh lemon juice
¼ teaspoon kosher salt

Garnish: Additional extra virgin olive oil; coarse salt

In a food processor or high-powered blender, add the yogurt, feta, water, olive oil, garlic, lemon juice and kosher salt. Process until very smooth and creamy, letting everything blend well for a couple minutes. Taste for seasoning. To add brightness and acidity, add more lemon juice. To mellow the tartness or thin out the dip, add a little more water or olive oil.

Transfer to a serving bowl and top with a drizzle of olive oil and a sprinkle of coarse salt. This will last for up to 5 days, covered and stored in the refrigerator.

I love to serve this creamy dip with crostini topped with Oven-Roasted Mini Sweet Peppers (page 150).

notes

Instead of Greek yogurt, you can substitute whipped cream cheese, crème fraîche or sour cream.

 Besides crudités platters, the romesco is delicious on a platter with grilled flank steak or salmon placed on top.

Bread-Free Romesco

Makes about 3 cups

- 2 red bell peppers or 1 (12-ounce) jar roasted red bell peppers, drained
- ¾ cup riced cauliflower, thawed if frozen
- 1 shallot, chopped
- 2 garlic cloves, roughly chopped
- 3 tablespoons sherry vinegar or red wine vinegar
- 3 tablespoons tomato paste
- ½ teaspoon paprika
- 2 tablespoons chopped fresh flat-leaf parsley
- 1½ cups almonds, toasted, salted or unsalted
- 2 to 3 tablespoons water
- 3 tablespoons extra virgin olive oil
- ½ teaspoon kosher salt
- Freshly ground black pepper

If you're using fresh bell peppers, roast them directly over a gas flame or on a sheet pan under a preheated broiler until charred all over. Seal in a paper bag to steam; let cool. Peel away the charred skin and remove the stems and seeds.

Roughly chop the roasted peppers. In a food processor, combine the roasted peppers, cauliflower, shallot, garlic, vinegar, tomato paste, paprika, parsley, almonds and 2 tablespoons water. Process until mostly smooth. With the machine on, pour in the olive oil. Season with the salt and pepper. If it seems too thick, thin it out with a little extra water. The romesco can be refrigerated for up to 3 days. Allow it to come to room temperature before serving.

notes

This is my take on a Catalonian condiment often served with fish and grilled meats. I use almonds as a binder instead of crusty bread or breadcrumbs, but you can use 1½ cups cubed dried crusty bread if you prefer. I add the cauliflower to sneak in vegetable bulk—often my secret weapon for getting more veggies into my kids. Omit the cauliflower if you don't have it on hand, since it doesn't change the flavor profile much. You can use regular paprika, but I love this with Pimentón de la Vera, which is smoked paprika used in paella.

 This vegan dip is full of protein, similar to hummus but without the added fat from tahini.

White Bean Dip with Rosemary Olive Oil

Makes about 2 cups

4 tablespoons extra virgin olive oil, divided
2 garlic cloves, roughly chopped
2 (15-ounce) cans cannellini or navy beans, drained and rinsed
Finely grated zest and juice of 1 lemon
2 tablespoons water
2 teaspoons kosher salt
¼ to ½ teaspoon crushed red pepper flakes
1 tablespoon fresh chopped rosemary leaves
Crackers, pita cut in bite-size pieces, endive spears or crudités, for serving

In a sauté pan over medium-high heat, heat 2 tablespoons of the olive oil. Add the garlic and stir until it's fragrant, being careful not to burn it, 1 minute or less. Transfer mixture to a high-powered blender or food processor and set the pan aside.

To the blender, add the beans, lemon zest and juice, water, salt and ¼ teaspoon of the red pepper flakes. Puree on high speed, until completely smooth. Place the dip in a serving bowl and set aside.

Return the sauté pan to medium heat and add the remaining 2 tablespoons olive oil and the rosemary. Heat the rosemary in the olive oil until fragrant, 2 to 3 minutes, stirring occasionally so it doesn't burn. Drizzle the olive oil and rosemary over the dip. Sprinkle with additional red pepper flakes, if desired. Serve warm or at room temperature with crackers, pita, crudités or endive. Store in an airtight container in the refrigerator for up to 3 days.

Change up the flavor here by topping the white bean dip with a swirl of olive tapenade or harissa paste.

Top to Bottom: Edamame Hummus, White Bean Dip with Rosemary Olive Oil, Simple Whipped Feta, Avocado-Jalapeño Green Goddess, Bread-Free Romesco,

 **SMART tip** Be sure to stir any separated oil into the tahini before using. I like to store my tahini upside down in the refrigerator so any separated oil ends up at the bottom; if you do this, just make sure the jar lid is on tight!

Edamame Hummus

Makes about 2 cups

¼ to ⅓ cup tahini

2 tablespoons extra virgin olive oil

1 or 2 garlic cloves, roughly chopped

2 cups shelled edamame, no need to steam

½ teaspoon kosher salt

Finely grated zest and juice of ½ lemon (about 1 tablespoon juice)

2 tablespoons water (optional)

½ cup packed fresh cilantro, parsley, chives and/or spinach leaves

In a food processor or high-powered blender, add the tahini, olive oil, garlic, edamame, salt, lemon zest and juice. Puree until smooth. If the mixture appears lumpy, add 2-3 tablespoons water and puree again. Add the herbs and/or spinach and pulse until they're chopped and well combined. Taste for salt and acidity and adjust if necessary.

Serve with crudités or pita chips.

Store in an airtight container in the refrigerator for up to 3 days.

 **notes**

If you are soy-free, substitute the edamame with an equal amount of drained and rinsed canned garbanzo beans or shelled fresh green peas.

 **SMART tip** Make sure the garbanzos are very dry before roasting to help them crisp up in the oven.

Spicy Roasted Garbanzos

Makes about 2 cups

- 2 (15-ounce) cans garbanzo beans, drained, rinsed and patted dry
- 2 tablespoons extra virgin olive oil or avocado oil
- 1 teaspoon ground cumin
- 1 teaspoon ground coriander
- 1 teaspoon ground chile powder
- ¼ teaspoon cayenne pepper, optional
- ½ teaspoon kosher salt
- Freshly ground black pepper
- Coarse salt, for finishing

Preheat the oven to 350 degrees. If you have a setting for convection roast, use that for crispier garbanzos.

In a medium bowl, toss the dry garbanzos with the olive oil, cumin, coriander, ground chile, optional cayenne pepper, salt and pepper. Spread in a single layer on a half sheet pan and roast for 60 minutes, checking on garbanzos after about 40 minutes. Remove the garbanzos from the oven when slightly crisp and golden brown. Finish with a little coarse salt. Serve warm or at room temperature. Before storing in an air tight container, make sure the garbanzos have completely cooled or the steam from the heat will soften them in the container.

I use these crispy beans on snack boards and as a gluten-free crouton alternative in salads. I love them in my Kale Caesar (page 28) or on top of hummus.

notes

Chili powder from the spice aisle is often a blend of spices such as dried chiles, cumin, garlic, onion and paprika. I prefer single varietal dried ground chiles, like ancho or arbol chile, but chile powder works fine.

 **SMART tip** Store packages of nuts in the freezer—they stay fresh much longer that way. The nuts we snack on nightly—like salty Marcona almonds—are stored in my pantry. If you don't have fresh rosemary and sage, use 3 tablespoons dried rosemary and omit the sage. You can cut the red pepper flakes in half if you don't like spice.

Cocktail Nuts with Rosemary and Sage

Makes about 3 cups

- 2 tablespoons extra virgin olive oil
- ¼ cup chopped fresh rosemary leaves (from about 6 large rosemary sprigs)
- About 20 fresh sage leaves, roughly torn
- 3 cups unsalted mixed nuts
- 2 teaspoons crushed red pepper flakes
- 2 teaspoons sugar
- 1 teaspoon garlic powder
- ½ teaspoon kosher salt

Over medium-high heat, heat the olive oil in a large skillet. Add the rosemary and sage and cook for 30 seconds or until the sizzling calms and the rosemary is just golden on the edges. Add the nuts, red pepper flakes, sugar, garlic powder and salt. Cook, stirring, until the nuts are fragrant. This should take 2 to 3 minutes. Transfer the nuts to a sheet pan to cool completely in a single layer. (This is an important step so that the nuts aren't piled up, making the bottom layer steam and soften.)

Alternatively, roast the nuts in a 400-degree oven. On a sheet pan, toss together all the ingredients and shake out into a single layer. Roast for about 12 to 15 minutes, until toasted and golden brown. Set aside to cool.

After the nuts are completely cool, store at room temperature in a paper towel-lined plastic or glass storage container with a tight-fitting lid.

notes

Make this with one type of nut, such as cashews or almonds, if you prefer. When friends give us Texas pecans from their ranches, I roast them using this recipe. They're great chopped and added to salads as a crunchy topping. During the holidays, these make a great gift for friends and neighbors.

SMART tip — PSA: Week-old eggs are easier to peel.

Deviled Eggs with Peas and Dill

Makes 24 deviled egg halves

12 large eggs
½ cup mayonnaise (I prefer Hellman's, Best Foods or Duke's)
1 tablespoon plus 1 teaspoon Dijon mustard
Pinch of cayenne pepper
¼ teaspoon kosher salt
Freshly ground black pepper
1 tablespoon minced fresh chives
1 tablespoon minced fresh dill
½ cup peas, thawed if frozen
Garnish: Additional minced fresh chives and dill

To cook the eggs, place them in a saucepan and cover with water by an inch or so. Bring to a boil over high heat. As soon as they come to a boil, remove from the heat, cover, and let stand for 12 minutes. Drain the eggs and rinse under cold water.

To peel the eggs, tap each egg on the counter all over to crack the shell, then roll the egg to loosen it. Peel while holding the egg under cool running water; this makes peeling easier and removes small pieces of shell stuck to the egg.

To make the filling, halve the eggs lengthwise. Carefully remove the yolks with a small spoon and add to a food processor or a mini prep food processor. Set the whites aside on a plate. Blend the yolks with the mayonnaise, mustard, cayenne, salt, pepper, chives and dill until smooth. Remove the blade and stir in the peas by hand.

Place the filling in a plastic bag and cut off a small portion of one corner. Pipe the filling into the whites. Garnish with additional herbs and serve immediately.

notes

You can also mix the filling by hand in a small bowl. Use a fork to mash the yolks and stir in the remaining ingredients to combine well. You may have filling left over. Don't toss it! Save it in the refrigerator for up to 5 days and use as a spread for toasted crusty bread or English muffins. Skip the peas and herbs if you want a traditional deviled egg. If you make the plain version, dress them up by adding a dollop of caviar for a special appetizer. Delicious paired with sparkling wine on New Year's Eve!

Dessert-*ish*

I don't make dessert during the week. It's a small miracle just to get dinner shopped for, prepped and made night after night.

And to be honest, no one needs the extra sugar and calories. But sometimes I decide to prep one of these recipes at night for a healthy treat or make-ahead breakfast. Take my Baked Oatmeal (page 196), for instance—topped with warm maple syrup it satisfies a sweet tooth. Or I'll make a batch of the Melting Moment cookie dough (page 204) that my mother-in-law's mom, Popo, would often make. Perfect with a cup of coffee in the morning. Grandma's Date Squares (page 200) can be snacked on after school or with an afternoon shot of espresso. My dad's mom would make them every Christmas and actually wrap the baking pan with a bow on top. I may not wrap them up like she did, but since she passed away my sister and I make them for my dad every December. Many of these recipes rely on healthy ingredients and add-ins like oats, chia seeds and berries, which helps me feel like they're just healthy enough.

192
Greek Yogurt and Berry Coffee Cake

194
Mixed Berry Crisp

196
Baked Oatmeal

198
Banana Snacking Cake

200
Grandma's Date Squares

202
Cranberry Streusel Muffins

204
Popo's Melting Moments

206
My Favorite Granola

208
Chia Seed Pudding

210
Chocolate, Almond and Banana Smoothie

SMART tip: I use applesauce in muffins and quick breads to cut down on the amount of butter or oil—it keeps baked goods moist without adding fat.

Greek Yogurt and Berry Coffee Cake

Serves 6

- Cooking spray
- 1½ cups all-purpose flour
- 1 teaspoon baking powder
- ¼ teaspoon baking soda
- ¼ teaspoon kosher salt
- 6 tablespoons unsalted butter, at room temperature
- ¾ cup sugar
- ½ cup applesauce
- 2 whole eggs or 3 egg whites
- 1 teaspoon vanilla extract
- 1¼ cup plain Greek yogurt
- 2 cups fresh blueberries, blackberries, raspberries or a combination
- 1 tablespoon plus 1 teaspoon turbinado or raw sugar, for sprinkling

Preheat the oven to 350 degrees. Coat an 8-inch square baking pan with cooking spray.

In a medium bowl, add the flour, baking powder, baking soda and salt; whisk well to combine. Set aside.

In a large bowl, use a handheld mixer to beat the butter and sugar until light and fluffy. Mix in applesauce. Add the eggs one at a time and beat to combine. Beat in the vanilla. Add the flour mixture and yogurt alternately to butter mixture, beginning and ending with the flour mixture. Scrape down the sides of the bowl as needed.

Lightly spoon half the batter into the baking pan. Spread half the berries over the batter, then spoon the remaining batter into the pan. Top with remaining berries. Sprinkle with the turbinado sugar. Bake for 50 to 60 minutes, until a cake tester inserted in the middle comes out clean. Serve warm or at room temperature.

Store leftovers in the refrigerator for up to 5 days. They're delicious slightly warmed in a microwave or toaster oven.

notes

To accurately measure flour, lightly spoon it into a dry measuring cup and level with the back of a knife. If you overpack flour, the finished outcome of your baked goods will be dry and dense. Instead of turbinado sugar, you can double the streusel topping from the Cranberry Streusel Muffins (page 202) and use it to top the coffee cake before baking.

SMART tip: To save yourself a bowl you'll have to wash later, mix the berry filling directly in the baking dish.

Mixed Berry Crisp

Serves 6

- ½ cup old-fashioned oats
- ½ cup all-purpose flour
- ½ cup packed light brown sugar
- ⅓ cup chopped pecans
- ⅛ teaspoon freshly grated nutmeg
- ¼ teaspoon ground cinnamon
- Generous pinch of salt
- 1 teaspoon vanilla extract
- 6 tablespoons cold unsalted butter, cut into ½-inch cubes
- 1½ cups fresh blueberries
- 1½ cups fresh blackberries
- 1½ cups fresh raspberries
- ¼ cup sugar
- ¼ teaspoon corn starch or arrowroot powder
- Juice of ½ lemon (about 1½ tablespoons)
- Whipped cream or vanilla ice cream, for serving

Preheat the oven to 375 degrees.

In a medium-size bowl, combine the oats, flour, brown sugar, pecans, nutmeg, cinnamon and salt. Sprinkle the vanilla on top and add the butter. Mix with your fingertips or a pastry blender until the topping comes together. There should not be any bits of flour or brown sugar left in the bowl; you should be left with creamy crumbles of topping. Set aside.

In a medium mixing bowl, add the blueberries, blackberries, raspberries, sugar, corn starch and lemon juice. Stir gently to combine.

Pour the berry mixture into an 8-inch square baking dish and sprinkle the topping evenly on top. Bake until golden and the filling is bubbling around the edges, about 45 minutes. Let cool for 5 minutes before serving. Top this fragrant crisp with a dollop of fresh whipped cream, or better yet, vanilla ice cream.

notes

Substitute other seasonal fruit, if you like—peaches, ripe nectarines and plums are all delicious here. I love the combination of blackberries and nectarines in a fruit crisp.

SMART tip For quick weekday breakfasts or a satisfying afternoon snack, leftovers can be reheated in the microwave for 30 seconds. It almost tastes like a warm oatmeal cookie!

Baked Oatmeal

Serves 4-6

- Cooking spray or 2 teaspoons butter
- 1½ cups quick-cooking or old-fashioned rolled oats (not steel-cut)
- 1 tablespoon chia seeds or chia powder
- 1 tablespoon flaxseed or ground flax
- 1 teaspoon ground cinnamon
- ⅛ teaspoon kosher salt
- ⅛ teaspoon freshly grated nutmeg
- ⅓ cup light or dark brown sugar, packed
- 1⅓ cup milk (skim, 2% or whole dairy; almond; soy; oat—whatever!)
- ¼ cup applesauce
- 1½ teaspoons vanilla extract
- ⅓ cup raisins, dried cranberries, dried cherries or dried blueberries

Toppings: Warmed maple syrup; Greek yogurt; an extra sprinkle of cinnamon; chopped nuts or sliced bananas or fresh berries, for serving

Preheat the oven to 350 degrees. Grease 6 individual ½-cup ramekins or an 8-inch square glass or ceramic baking dish with cooking spray or butter.

In a medium bowl, add the oats, chia, flax, cinnamon, salt, nutmeg, brown sugar, milk, applesauce, vanilla and fruit. Stir well to combine. Pour into the prepared dish and smooth out the top layer. Bake for 25 minutes or until set. The center of the baked oatmeal should be slightly firm to the touch.

Serve warm on its own or with the toppings you prefer.

You can assemble this ahead and store it unbaked, covered, in the refrigerator overnight.

notes

I sometimes add a grated tart baking apple (no need to peel) to the batter. Or bake with about ½ cup of fresh blueberries on the top, just lightly push them into the batter. Use gluten-free oats if you like, or a dairy-free milk. You can replace the applesauce with ¼ cup mashed banana.

SMART tip Instead of a square pan, you can also bake this for the same amount of time in a traditional loaf pan to make banana bread. When my bananas start to turn brown and then black, I put them in a freezer bag and toss them in my freezer. That way I'm always prepared to make this cake!

Banana Snacking Cake

Serves 4-6

- 1 cup unsalted butter, at room temperature, plus more for greasing pan
- 1½ cups all-purpose flour
- 1½ teaspoons baking soda
- 1 teaspoon ground cinnamon
- ½ teaspoon kosher salt
- 1 cup sugar
- 1 teaspoon vanilla extract
- 2 eggs, at room temperature
- ½ cup well-shaken buttermilk
- 3-4 very ripe bananas with black skins, mashed (1 to 1½ cups)
- **Optional:** 1 soft but not overripe banana, peel on, and turbinado sugar, for sprinkling

Preheat the oven to 350 degrees. Grease an 8- or 9-inch square baking pan with butter. Line the bottom of the pan with parchment paper, creasing the inside edge so it fits snugly into the pan. Let two sides of the parchment paper hang over the pan, which will help you remove it easily later. Grease the parchment as well.

In a medium bowl, add the flour, baking soda, cinnamon and salt; whisk well to combine. Set aside.

In a large bowl with a handheld mixer, beat the butter on medium speed for about a minute; use a rubber spatula to scrape down the inside of the bowl. With the mixer running on medium to medium-high speed, slowly pour in the sugar in a steady stream. Continue beating for 3 to 5 minutes, until very light and fluffy and a light yellow color, stopping to scrape down the sides of the bowl about halfway through. Add the vanilla, then add the eggs one at a time, completely incorporating each egg. Turn the mixer to low speed and pour in one-third of the flour mixture, one-third of the buttermilk and one-third of the mashed bananas. Repeat until all the dry ingredients, buttermilk and bananas are incorporated. Pour the batter into the prepared pan.

To top with the optional banana slices before baking, gently slice the banana in half lengthwise with its peel on. This will make it less likely that the banana will break in half. Carefully remove the peel and place each slice cut side up, gently push into the batter, leaving about 2 inches of space between the halves. Sprinkle the banana with turbinado sugar.

Bake for about 70 to 90 minutes, until a cake tester inserted in the center comes out mostly clean. Check after 30 minutes, covering the pan with foil if the cake is getting too brown. Remove from the oven and let cool on a wire rack. Once mostly cool to the touch, you can lift the cake out of the pan using the overhanging parchment paper.

Store in the refrigerator for up to 4 days.

notes

Instead of baking the banana halves into the top of the cake, you can make a glaze by mixing together 1 tablespoon buttermilk and 1 cup powdered sugar. Drizzle on top of the cake after it bakes. Try adding ½ cup chocolate chips to the batter or to the top of the cake before baking.

SMART tip: These are a traditional Canadian bar cookie, sometimes called matrimonial bars, that my Grandma Whyte would make during the holidays. Store in an airtight container in the refrigerator for up to a week.

Grandma's Date Squares

Makes about 25 squares

Filling
- ¼ cup packed light brown sugar
- ½ teaspoon ground cinnamon
- ¼ teaspoon freshly grated nutmeg
- Finely grated zest and juice of 1 large orange (about ½ cup juice)
- ¼ teaspoon kosher salt
- 2 cups pitted dates (preferably Medjool; about a 12-ounce package)
- 3 tablespoons water
- 1½ teaspoons vanilla extract

Crust
- 2 cups old-fashioned oats
- 1 cup all-purpose flour
- 1 cup packed light brown sugar
- 1½ teaspoons ground cinnamon
- ⅛ teaspoon freshly grated nutmeg
- ½ teaspoon baking powder
- ½ teaspoon kosher salt
- 12 tablespoons cold unsalted butter, cubed
- 1½ teaspoons vanilla extract

Preheat the oven to 350 degrees. Grease an 8-inch square baking pan. Line the bottom of the pan with parchment paper, creasing the inside edge so it fits snugly into the pan. Let two sides of the parchment paper hang over the pan, which will help you easily remove it later on. Grease the parchment as well.

Filling: In a small saucepan over medium heat, add the brown sugar, cinnamon, nutmeg, orange zest and juice and salt; stir until the sugar is melted. Reduce the heat to low and add the dates and water. Use a wooden spoon or a potato masher to break up the dates and mash them into a thick paste. Stir in the vanilla and cook uncovered for 2 minutes or until the dates are tender and mashed. Set aside.

Crust: In a large bowl, combine the oats, flour, brown sugar, cinnamon, nutmeg, baking powder and salt. Using a pastry blender or two knives, cut in the butter until the mixture is crumbly. Add the vanilla. Use your fingers to bring the dough together until it forms large clumps. There shouldn't be dry flour left in the bowl.

Press half of the dough into the baking pan. Carefully spread the date mixture on top. Sprinkle the remaining dough in bits over the filling to create a crumbly topping. Bake for 30 minutes or until golden. Cool in the pan on a wire rack. When completely cooled, gently remove the parchment paper from the pan and place on a cutting board to cut into small squares with a serrated knife.

notes

Fresh Medjool dates are found either in the produce section usually found near the fresh cheeses. I store them in the refrigerator. They are my go-to afternoon snack when I'm craving something sweet, even better with almond butter and a sprinkle of salt on top. If you can't find fresh dates, use the dried dates that are found usually near dried apricots and raisins. When using dried dates, add ½ cup water along with the spices and orange juice and they will soften up in the saucepan.

SMART tip Be sure to spoon the flour into dry measuring cups, or lightly scoop and level. Mix the batter until just combined to ensure the flour doesn't get overworked. Otherwise you might end up with dry and dense muffins!

Cranberry Streusel Muffins

Makes about 12 muffins

Muffin Batter
2 cups all-purpose flour
2 tablespoons chia seeds
1 teaspoon ground cinnamon
2 teaspoons baking powder
½ teaspoon kosher salt
½ cup unsalted butter, at room temperature
1 cup sugar
2 large eggs
1 teaspoon almond extract
½ cup milk (skim, 2% or whole)
1 cup dried cranberries

Streusel Topping
¼ cup packed light brown sugar
¼ cup sliced almonds
2 tablespoons all-purpose flour
1 teaspoon ground cinnamon
2 tablespoons unsalted butter, melted
Pinch of kosher salt

Glaze
1 cup powdered sugar
1 tablespoon water
¼ teaspoon almond extract

Preheat the oven to 350 degrees. Line a 12-cup muffin tin with paper cups.

Muffin Batter: In a medium bowl, whisk together the flour, chia seeds, cinnamon, baking powder and salt. Set aside.

In a large bowl, use a handheld mixer to beat the butter and sugar until fluffy. Beat in the eggs, one at a time. Add the almond extract and mix to combine.

Either with a handheld mixer on the lowest speed or by hand, add the flour mixture to the butter mixture, alternating with the milk, in three batches until just combined. Mix until the flour is mostly combined, but the batter doesn't need to be smooth. Gently fold in the cranberries by hand until just incorporated. Spoon the batter into the muffin cups; they will be very full.

Streusel Topping: In a small bowl combine the brown sugar, sliced almonds, flour and cinnamon. Pour in the melted butter and stir to combine. Make sure the streusel clumps up into small pieces when pressed between your fingers. Sprinkle the streusel on top of the muffins.

Bake muffins in the center of the oven for 25 minutes, until a tester inserted into the center comes out clean. Let the muffins cool in the pan for 5 minutes, and then transfer to a wire rack to cool.

Glaze: In a small bowl, combine the powdered sugar, water and almond extract and stir until smooth. Use a spoon to drizzle a little of the glaze over the top of each muffin. Store the muffins at room temperature in an airtight container for up to 3 days or freeze for up to a month.

notes

I like to use a silicone muffin pan to make these; coat the inside lightly with cooking spray and the muffins pop right out after cooling. If you're in a hurry, skip the streusel topping and glaze. Use halved pitted cherries in season instead of dried cranberries.

SMART tip — The unbaked dough can be refrigerated for up to 2 weeks or frozen up to 3 months. I like to keep a batch of this dough in the freezer to slice and bake as needed. These are delicious warm with an afternoon coffee or tea.

Popo's Melting Moments

Makes about 20 cookies

1 cup unsalted butter, at room temperature
½ cup powdered sugar
1¾ cups all-purpose flour
¼ cup corn starch
Pinch of kosher salt
1 teaspoon vanilla extract

In a large bowl, use a handheld mixer to beat the butter and powdered sugar until light and fluffy, 2 to 3 minutes. Add the flour, corn starch and salt and mix on low until just combined. Add the vanilla and mix to combine.

Turn out dough onto a large piece of plastic wrap. Form it into a 10×2-inch log of dough. Wrap well in the plastic. Chill the dough for 30 minutes in the freezer or 1 hour in the refrigerator before slicing and baking.

When you're ready to bake, preheat the oven to 375 degrees. Line a half sheet pan with parchment paper.

Cut the log of dough into ½-inch slices and place on the prepared pan. Bake until the cookies are slightly brown on the edges, 10 to 12 minutes. Remove from the oven and transfer to a wire rack to cool and enjoy warm or at room temperature. Store cookies in an airtight container at room temperature.

notes

Popo is my mother-in-law's mom, and she's famous for these cookies. I've made these with gluten-free baking flour, such as Cup4Cup, and they turn out great. You can roll the cookie dough log in crystallized sugar and slice before baking.

 **SMART tip** Lift the long sides of the parchment paper to slide the cooled granola into a storage container. It's a lot more efficient than using a spoon!

My Favorite Granola

Makes 8 cups

3 cups old-fashioned oats
1 cup unsweetened flaked coconut
1 cup roughly chopped pecans or pecan pieces
1 cup hulled raw pumpkin seeds (pepitas)
¼ cup avocado oil or extra virgin olive oil
¾ teaspoon kosher salt
½ cup maple syrup
3 tablespoons molasses
1 teaspoon ground cinnamon
½ teaspoon ground ginger
½ teaspoon freshly grated nutmeg
1 teaspoon vanilla extract
1 cup roughly chopped candied ginger
1 cup dried cranberries, raisins or cherries
Fresh berries, yogurt and honey, for serving

Preheat the oven to 300 degrees. Line two half sheet pans with parchment paper.

In a large bowl, add the oats, coconut, pecans, pepitas, oil, salt, maple syrup, molasses, cinnamon, ground ginger, nutmeg and vanilla. Mix well to combine.

On the prepared sheet pans, spread the granola out in a single layer. Bake for 35 minutes or until golden brown. I don't flip or stir the granola while it cooks because I like it clumpy, but stir it halfway through if you prefer.

Remove from the oven and sprinkle the candied ginger and cranberries evenly over the top. When the granola has completely cooled, transfer to an airtight container and store at room temperature for up to a week. (Don't store before the granola is cool—it will get soft!)

notes

The granola won't get as crispy if it's heaped onto the pan, so be sure it's spread in a single layer. You can omit the molasses to make this slightly less rich. Omit the candied ginger if you're not a fan.

SMART tip — These are a protein-rich breakfast or afternoon treat that's similar in texture to rice pudding. It's best with one of the slightly sweet toppings, like berries or banana slices.

Chia Seed Pudding

Makes 5-10 puddings

½ cup white or black chia seeds
2 cups unsweetened vanilla almond milk
2 tablespoons honey, light agave nectar or maple syrup
½ teaspoon vanilla extract
Pinch of kosher salt
Toppings: Berries; kiwi slices; banana slices; coconut flakes; sliced almonds

In a large mixing bowl, whisk together the chia seeds, almond milk, honey, vanilla and salt until well combined. Let the mixture sit for about 5 minutes to thicken.

Stir again. Use a ladle or measuring cup with a spout to portion the pudding into mason jars, glass cups or small bowls. Give the pudding a quick stir in between filling the containers to redistribute the chia seeds. Refrigerate at least 6 hours or overnight, until it sets. Garnish as you like when serving.

The ungarnished puddings, covered with a lid or plastic wrap, will last up to 4 to 5 days in the refrigerator.

notes

Chia seeds are full of fiber, protein and antioxidants. They contain a natural pectin that gets gelatinous when mixed with liquid. I prefer this with the homemade vanilla almond milk on my blog, but store-bought works, too!

 Adding just one Brazil nut to a smoothie will fulfill your daily recommended intake of selenium, which helps regulate hormones.

Chocolate, Almond and Banana Smoothie

Makes 1 or 2 smoothies

¾ cup unsweetened vanilla almond milk or water

1 ripe banana (fresh or frozen), peeled and chopped

2 heaping tablespoons almond butter

2 shelled Brazil nuts

2 pitted Medjool dates

1 tablespoon chia seeds

2 teaspoons cacao powder

2 teaspoons hemp hearts

½ cup ice (about 6 cubes)

In a high-powered blender, combine all the ingredients. Puree well. Thin with additional water or almond milk if you like.

notes

Chia adds fiber, which keeps you full, as well as omega-3s. Cacao powder is an unsweetened, raw and unroasted form of cocoa powder. Hemp hearts are high in protein and heart-healthy omega-6 and omega-3 fatty acids. Store all your smoothie add-ins in the freezer and they will last twice as long. You could also add a teaspoon of Maca powder, an Incan cruciferous vegetable, said to help balance hormones and boost mood and energy.

Cocktails

My approach to cocktails is pretty basic.

Conjure up the opposite of a tattooed bartender who whips up complicated elixirs. That's what we have here! Simple recipes you can make at home without a ton of steps. Made from citrus and fruit, fragrant herbs and good-quality components, which is really all you need!

There's nothing like an evening at home that starts with a good cocktail. A refreshing libation can make a Friday night at home feel like date night.

There are a few pieces of equipment and ingredients that are helpful to have on hand; I've outlined those here. Stock your bar and send out the invites, it's time to Don Draper.

216 Cocktails 101

218 Fresh Grapefruit Paloma

220 Ginger Margarita

221 Aperol Margarita

222 Big-Batch Jalapeño Margaritas

224 Summer Sangria (Peach-Prosecco Punch)

Winter Sangria

226 Strawberry Bourbon Smash

226 Hot Honey Bees Knees

Pineapple Rum Punch

228 Negroni Sbagliato

Sorbet-Prosecco Spritz (Sgroppino)

Campari, OJ and Soda

Cocktails 101

- **Salt for rims:** You want to use good salt, just like when you're cooking. Don't use iodized table salt! Kosher salt is great; Himalayan salt adds a pretty pink rim. You can also play around with smoked salts or volcanic salts.
- **You don't need to salt the entire rim of a margarita glass.** Go halfsies by dipping just one side of the rim in liquid and salt. That way, you don't need to ask every guest what they prefer. Everyone will have a spot to sip with salt or without.
- **Glasses are a personal preference and I'll leave those up to you.** I sometimes use our everyday water glasses to make cocktails. Plus, I love to buy antique glassware when I find it.
- **Agave nectar is an optional sweetener in margaritas; you can leave it out.** You'll end up with a slightly tarter cocktail, but without the added calories. You can use agave nectar instead of simple syrup in almost any cocktail recipe.
- **When I make a spritzer or add sparkling water to cocktails,** I use whatever we have on hand, from Pellegrino or Topo Chico to regular club soda.
- **When a recipe calls for Prosecco,** you can substitute any sparkling wine, such as Champagne, crémant or cava.
- **Most cocktail recipes call for ounce measurements,** but I use tablespoon and cup measures to be consistent with my other recipes.

Tools

Cocktail shaker

Mason jars (can be used as shakers, and as cocktail glasses once the lids are removed)

Bar spoon with a long handle

Muddler

Pitcher

Small strainer

Ice molds

Ice mallet and bag kit, for DIY crushed ice

Small liquid measures or a jigger

Liquors and Mixers

Tequila (I use blanco or silver)

Aperol and Campari

Rum

Whiskey or Bourbon

Freshly-squeezed citrus juice is always my first pick

Sweet Red Vermouth

Ginger Beer

Aperol Margarita

 **SMART tip** Using Himalayan salt or Redmond Real Salt makes for a colorful pink rim.

Fresh Grapefruit Paloma

Makes 1 or 2 cocktails

Salted Rim (optional)
¼ cup kosher salt
½ teaspoon finely grated lime or grapefruit zest
Water, fresh lime juice or grapefruit juice

Cocktail
¼ cup fresh grapefruit juice
1 tablespoon fresh lime juice
1 teaspoon light agave nectar
¼ cup blanco or silver tequila
Ice cubes
¼ cup club soda or sparkling water
Garnish: Rosemary sprig; 4 to 5 jalapeño chile slices; grapefruit wedge

If you like a salted rim, add the salt to a small plate. To add color and flavor, if you like, stir in the lime or grapefruit zest. Add the water to a second plate. Dip the rim of the cocktail glass in the liquid and then the salt. Set aside.

In a cocktail shaker, add the grapefruit and lime juices, agave, tequila and a scoop of ice. Shake very well for 20 seconds or so. Remove the lid and transfer to a glass; I don't strain because I prefer the extra ice from the cocktail shaker. Add more fresh ice, top off with club soda and stir. Finish with an optional garnish.

You can also make the cocktail directly in salt-rimmed (or not) glasses: Add the grapefruit and lime juices and agave and stir until the agave is incorporated. Add the tequila, ice and club soda and stir.

Big Batch: To make 6 cocktails, in a pitcher combine 1½ cups grapefruit juice, ⅓ cup lime juice, 2 tablespoons agave and 1½ cups tequila. Stir well. Pour into individual ice-filled glasses and top off with club soda.

 **notes**
I prefer the lighter flavor of silver tequila, but reposado works as well. If you're a mezcal fan, give that a try.

Left to Right: Aperol Margarita, Ginger Margarita, Fresh Grapefruit Paloma

 **SMART tip** If you love the flavor of ginger, add some finely grated fresh ginger to the salted rim.

Ginger Margarita

Makes 1 or 2 cocktails

Salted Rim (optional)
¼ cup kosher salt
½ teaspoon finely grated lime zest (optional)
Water or fresh lime juice

Cocktail
¼ cup fresh lime juice, divided
¼ cup blanco or silver tequila
1 tablespoon light agave nectar
Ice cubes
⅓ cup ginger beer
Garnish: 1 or 2 lime slices

If you like a salted rim, add the salt to a small plate. To add color and flavor, if you like, stir in the lime zest. Add the water to a second plate. Dip the rim of the cocktail glass in the liquid and then the salt. Set aside.

In a cocktail shaker, add the tequila, lime juice, agave nectar and a scoop of ice. Shake well for about 20 seconds. (Don't add the ginger beer to the cocktail shaker or the shaker will explode!) Remove the lid and transfer to an ice-filled glass. I don't strain because I prefer the extra ice from the cocktail shaker. Add the ginger beer and stir. Garnish with a lime slice.

You can also stir together the tequila, lime juice, agave nectar and ginger beer directly in a salt-rimmed glass, then add ice. When I use a shaker, I like the shards of ice that end up in the cocktail.

Big Batch: To make 6 cocktails, in a large pitcher combine 1½ cups blanco or silver tequila, 1½ cups fresh lime juice, ⅓ cup light agave nectar and 2 cups ginger beer and mix well. Serve over ice.

 **notes**
Since ginger beer is non-alcoholic, you can make this into a refreshing mocktail by eliminating the tequila.

 **SMART tip** For a slightly less sweet version, try making this with Campari instead.

Aperol Margarita

Makes 1 or 2 cocktails

Salted Rim (optional)
¼ cup kosher salt
½ teaspoon finely grated lime zest (optional)
Water or fresh lime juice

Cocktail
3 tablespoons blanco or silver tequila
2 tablespoons Aperol
2 tablespoons fresh lime juice
1 tablespoon fresh orange juice
1 tablespoon light agave nectar
Ice cubes
¼ cup club soda
Garnish: Orange slice

If you like a salted rim, add the salt to a small plate. To add color and flavor, if you like, stir in the lime zest. Add the water to a second plate. Dip the rim of the cocktail glass in the liquid and then the salt. Set aside.

In a cocktail shaker, add the tequila, Aperol, lime and orange juices, and agave along with a scoop of ice. Cover and shake well for about 20 seconds. Strain over fresh ice into a cocktail glass and add the club soda. Serve topped with an orange slice.

Big Batch: To make 20 cocktails, in a large pitcher combine 3¾ cups blanco or silver tequila, 2½ cups Aperol, 2½ cups fresh lime juice, 1¼ cups fresh orange juice and 1¼ cups light agave nectar. Stir well. This can be made up to a day ahead, then covered and chilled. When you're ready to serve, stir well and pour into ice-filled glasses. Top off each with ¼ cup club soda and stir. (Don't be tempted to add the club soda ahead of time; you want it to stay bubbly.)

 **notes**
Since these contain both tequila and Aperol, they have slightly more alcohol. Consider yourself warned!

 **SMART tip** Make this one day ahead for slightly spicy margaritas—and two days ahead if you like more heat!

Big-Batch Jalapeño Margaritas

Makes about 12 cocktails

2 jalapeño chiles, thinly sliced (no need to seed)
3 cups blanco or silver tequila
3¼ cups fresh lime juice, divided
1 tablespoon Tajin spice mix
½ cup light agave nectar
Ice cubes
About 3 cups club soda or sparkling water
Garnish: Fresh jalapeño slices

In a pitcher, add the jalapeño slices and their seeds to the tequila. Cover and set aside. Let the tequila infuse at room temperature for at least 6 hours or up to 2 days.

When you're ready to serve, in a small dish add ¼ cup of the lime juice. In another small dish, add the Tajin. Dip the rims of the glasses in the lime juice, then in the Tajin. Stir the agave nectar and the remaining 3 cups lime juice into the infused tequila. Fill 12 (10-ounce) glasses with ice. Pour in the margarita mixture and top with club soda. (To avoid the jalapeño seeds, use a cocktail strainer when filling the glasses.)

notes

If you don't have time to infuse the tequila or for a non-spicy version, omit the jalapeños and combine the remaining ingredients in a pitcher.

SMART tip — Brandy is a traditional sangria addition, but this has a lighter flavor if you leave it out. You can make this a day ahead and chill. Combine everything except the prosecco and mint, which needs to be added just before serving.

Winter Sangria

Serves 6 to 8

3 tangerines, 1 small navel orange or 1 blood orange, thinly sliced (no need to peel)
1 (750 ml) bottle prosecco
3 cups pomegranate juice
¼ cup brandy or cognac
1 cup pomegranate seeds
1 pear, cored and thinly sliced (no need to peel)
½ cup seedless green or red grapes, halved
2 cinnamon sticks
2 star anise

Combine all ingredients in a large pitcher and stir to combine. Serve in ice-filled wine glasses, making sure to include some of the fruit.

Summer Sangria
(Peach-Prosecco Punch)

Serves 6 to 8

2 fresh nectarines or peaches, sliced (no need to peel)
½ cup fresh blueberries or blackberries
1 lemon, thinly sliced
1 (750 ml) bottle prosecco
3 cups peach nectar or juice
¼ cup brandy or cognac (optional)
Garnish: Fresh mint flowers and leaves

In a large pitcher or punch bowl, add the nectarines, berries, lemon, prosecco and peach nectar. Add the brandy, if you like. Stir gently. Serve in ice-filled wine glasses, making sure to include some of the fruit; garnish with mint.

Strawberry-Bourbon Smash

Makes 1 cocktail

3 fresh strawberries, hulled
4 fresh basil leaves
¼ cup bourbon or whiskey
3 tablespoons fresh lemon juice

Ice cubes
¼ cup ginger beer
Garnish: Fresh basil or strawberry

In a cocktail shaker, use a muddler to mash the strawberries and basil. Add the bourbon, lemon juice and a scoop of ice. Secure the lid and shake well, about 20 seconds. Strain the cocktail into a cocktail glass filled with fresh ice. Stir in ginger beer and garnish with basil or a strawberry.

I also like an unstrained version of this cocktail with chunky pieces of fruit and bits of muddled herbs, but it can be tricky to drink. The strained version is a bit more refined!

Hot Honey Bees Knees

Makes 4 cocktails

1 cup gin
¼ cup honey
¼ cup fresh lemon juice
¼ teaspoon crushed red pepper flakes, optional

Ice cubes
Garnish: Lemon zest, fresh rosemary or thyme sprigs

Add the gin, honey, lemon juice, red pepper flakes (if using) and a scoop of ice to a cocktail shaker. Cover and shake well to combine, about 20 seconds. Strain into chilled coupe glasses and garnish with lemon zest, rosemary or a thyme sprig.

Pineapple Rum Punch

Makes 1 to 2 cocktails

¼ cup fresh grapefruit juice
¼ cup pineapple juice
3 tablespoons rum (I use Jamaican rum)
1 teaspoon fresh lime juice

Dash of Angostura bitters or grenadine
Ice cubes
Garnish: Lime wedge; fresh mint flowers

In a cocktail shaker, add the grapefruit juice, pineapple juice, rum, lime juice and bitters, along with a scoop of ice. Shake well for about 20 seconds. Strain into a cocktail glass filled with fresh ice and garnish with a lime wedge.

Left to Right: Hot Honey Bees Knees, Pineapple Rum Punch, Strawberry Bourbon Smash

SMART tip — Campari can be slightly bitter; add more prosecco if you want to lighten the flavor.

Negroni Sbagliato

Makes 1 cocktail

Ice cubes
2 tablespoons sweet red vermouth
2 tablespoons Campari
¼ cup prosecco
Garnish: Orange slice or twist

In an ice-filled cocktail glass, stir together the vermouth and Campari. Top with the prosecco and stir to combine. Garnish with an orange slice or twist.

Sorbet-Prosecco Spritz (Sgroppino)

Makes 1 cocktail

1 scoop lemon sorbet
½ cup prosecco
Garnish (optional): Fresh thyme sprigs or thinly sliced mint leaves

In a coupe glass or wine glass, add the sorbet. Add the prosecco and garnish with the thyme, if using. Serve immediately, with a spoon.

Campari, OJ and Soda

Makes 1 or 2 cocktails

¼ cup Campari
¼ cup fresh orange juice
½ cup club soda or sparkling water
Ice cubes

In a cocktail shaker, stir together the Campari, orange juice and club soda. Pour into one or two ice-filled cocktail glasses.

Negroni Sbagliato, Sorbet-Prosecco Spritz, Campari, OJ and Soda

Kitchen Equipment 101

Equipment isn't the end-all-be-all. That said, it can help make your cooking easier and better. My favorite cooking tools—the ones I use most often—are my citrus press, Microplane, bench scraper and pastry blender. For more details on kitchen tools and where to find them, scan the QR code on the next page and it will take you to my website.

Knives
Chef's knife
Serrated bread knife
Paring knife
Mandoline or handheld slicer

Three good knives. That's really all you need. A chef's knife, a serrated bread knife and a paring knife. Keep them sharp and they will last you a lifetime. I hone my knives with a sharpening steel at home and take them to get professionally sharpened twice a year.

I always get asked what brand of knives I recommend, but it's really a personal preference. Go shopping and hold several chef's knives in your hand. Opt for an 8- or 9-inch chef's knife that's comfortable for you to hold and can be resharpened, not one of those knives sold door to door that are all serrated—just say no. (I love their kitchen shears, though!)

Cutting Boards
Wooden boards
Wood board oil or food-grade mineral oil
Large carving board with a moat, for cutting meats

I prefer wooden boards because they're kinder to the blade of your chef's knife, and I just love their texture and look. Wash them with warm soapy water and dry well; and oil with food-grade mineral oil or "board oil" them occasionally, and they will last you a long time. Never soak them in water or put them in the dishwasher. After I wash and dry mine, I stand them up on the thin edge to continue drying; if you lay them down flat while damp, they will warp over time.

Cooking Pots and Pans
Cast-iron skillet
Grill pan
Nonstick skillet (I use ceramic nonstick)
8- or 10-inch frying pan
3-quart sauté pan with lid
4-quart pot with lid for soups and pasta
Small and medium soup pots
Small medium saucepans
8-quart stockpot with lid
Wok or large high-sided sauté pan
Dutch oven

Baking and Roasting Equipment
Half sheet pans (with rim)
Quarter sheet pans (with rim)
Roasting pan with a flat rack
Ceramic casserole pan
Bundt pan
9-inch round cake pans
8-inch square baking pan
8-inch square glass or ceramic baking dish
9×13-inch baking pan
9×13-inch ceramic baking dish
Ceramic baking dish
Small baking dish
Loaf pan
Silpat (silicone baking mat) or parchment paper
Silicone muffin pan
Wire cooling rack

Measuring Cups and Spoons

Liquid measuring cups with a spout

Dry measuring cups with a flat rim

Measuring spoons with an elongated bowl so they will fit in spice jars.

Mise en Place and Prep

Colanders

Strainers

Box grater

Microplane

Stacking prep bowls (glass and stainless steel)

Small prep bowls

Bench scraper

Pepper mill

Storage containers with tight-fitting lids, for stashing leftovers (I prefer glass)

Grilling

Long tongs

Grill brush

Silicone basting brush

Large grill spatula

For Meat and Seafood Cooking

Instant-read meat thermometer

Butcher twine

Parchment paper cooking bags

Fish spatula

Appliances

Vitamix or other high-powered blender

Immersion blender

Slow cooker

Instant Pot or pressure cooker

Food processor

Mini prep food processor

Handheld or stand mixer

Miscellaneous Tools

Wooden spoons

Whisks

Tongs

Pastry blender

Citrus press

Slotted spoons

Wooden salad bowl

Rubber spatula

Mixing bowls

I don't use a garlic press; I find it faster and less messy to smash and roughly chop garlic with a chef's knife.

Scan this QR code for a link to a list of my kitchen equipment favorites. You will also find helpful information on the best way to use many kitchen tools as well as more of my favorite recipes for you to try.

Acknowledgments

I'm not quite sure where to begin. This book wouldn't be here without the support and help of so many. My heart explodes to think of the family members, friends, cooking class students and blog readers who cheered me on along the way. This project was originally slated to begin photography just as the Covid pandemic hit. When we had to hit pause, I panicked that it would never happen. But the time spent cooking at home gave birth to new recipes and a new perspective.

First and foremost, I need to thank my sweet husband, **Brig**, whose mantra is "make it happen." He is my rock. Thank you to **my children** who tasted so many of these recipes and helped load and unload my car with groceries and props on photography days, and then ate the leftovers from the photography shoots for countless dinners. And also for having patience and understanding that Mom was a little distracted during the making of this book. My parents, **Karen** and **Jerry Whyte**, and my in-laws, **Patrice** and **Skip Smart**, who gave good feedback and encouragement. There's not a grocery store check-out clerk from North Carolina to California who doesn't know about this book, thanks to my mom.

What can I say about "The Dream Team." This project had the best photographer, designer and editor anyone could ask for. **Debora Smail**, **René** and **Timothy**, thank you for peaceful and creative studio days full of inspirational quotes, tacos and Leon Bridges. **Elise DeSilva**, thank you for designing the most beautiful book I've ever seen. This is exactly what I dreamed it would look and feel like; we are sympatico! And **Roni Atnipp**, who didn't give up on me and continued a conversation that started years ago, and here we are! We did it! You have forever improved my recipe writing. **Suzanne Fass**, **Suzanne Garofalo**, **Raquel Segal** and **Susan Thompson**, who made the book a lot more literate. And thank you to the whole team at **LIMB** and **Bayside Printing**.

Melissa Garlington, who kept things afloat at Smart in the Kitchen and organized all the recipe testing, tested countless recipes herself and gave valuable feedback. **Karen Fergus**, who prepped like a pro and helped me cook up a storm on studio days. And my Kinkaid School interns, **Johana Castro** and **Brooke Martin**, who taught me how to use Google docs and test every recipe start to finish. **Katherine Joe**, for her professional recipe testing notes, as well as volunteer recipe testers **Leslie Blanton**, **Kathy Boyett**, **Kristen Buck**, **Susan Cox**, **Elaine Day**, **Kimberley De Frantes**,

Miroma Photography

Mother's Day 2011, Paige (3), Brody (5) and Avery (8)

Marian Dresser, Catherine Fox, Melissa Garlington, Scott Garlington, Lori Gobillot, Pamela Hutchinson, Martha Justice, Gina Lamme, Heather Lingle, Katherine Lucke, Meg Moehle, Karen Stopnicki, Betsy Striegler, Mauri Tardy, Heather Whitfield and Laurie Sellers.

Sincere gratitude to ALL the students in my membership group, **Smart in the Kitchen School**, who listened to me talk about this project for years during classes and got excited for me! I'm so thankful for your support.

Dinora Segura, owner of **Great Expectations Cleaning**, who said she would help and support me with whatever I needed during the book process! And her amazing team, especially **Christina Ruano** and **Rosa Ramírez**, who helped me wash extra dishes, and more dishes, and yet more dishes.

Victoria Callaway, with **VCI Artists**, who helped me feel great on the cover shoot day even though I was so nervous to be in the photos!

Rita Joubran who supplied me with her delicious **Old Country Olive Oil** for recipe testing and photography. And **Kimberly Dorris** from **KD Weave** who supplied her woven textiles for photography props.

And also **my wonderful friends** who didn't forget about me when I dropped off the face of the earth to work on a book. While writing this, my oldest was a senior in high school and going through the college application process, my son was working towards (fingers crossed) his Eagle Scout and my youngest was navigating middle school. There are too many moms who helped me out in some way to possibly list here. I love you all.

It's difficult to explain the amount of work and "blood, sweat and tears" that goes into making a cookbook. It's not a literary novel by any means, but I wanted the writing to be good. And, most of all, I wanted you to use this.

So to any of you who pick up this book and cook a recipe, or recommend the book to a friend, thank you from the bottom of my heart.

* **Photographs** are indicated in boldface.

A
Agave nectar, 216
- Aperol Margarita, **217**, **219**, 221
- Big-Batch Jalapeño Margaritas, 222, **223**
- Ginger Margarita, **219**, 220

Almond milk
- Chia Seed Pudding, 208, **209**
- Chocolate, Almond and Banana Smoothie, 210, **211**

Almonds
- "Any Greens" Pesto Pasta, 48, **49**
- Bread-Free Romesco, 179, **181**
- Cranberry Streusel Muffins, 202, **203**
- Roasted Zucchini with Marcona Almond–Rosemary Crunch, 156, **157**

Anchovies
- Broccolini with Lemon Vinaigrette, 146, **147**
- Kale Caesar, 28, **29**
- Red Snapper Roasted with Italian Salsa Verde, 86, **87**

"Any Greens" Pesto Pasta, 48, **49**
- Parchment Paper Fish Packets, 84, **85**

Aperol, **217**, **219**, 221
Aperol Margarita, **217**, **219**, 221

Apple cider vinegar
- Red Cabbage Slaw, 32, **33**
- Super Simple Salad Dressing, 40, **41**

Apples
- Collard Greens and Brussels Sprout Salad, 26, **27**

Applesauce
- Greek Yogurt and Berry Coffee Cake, 192, **193**

Arugula
- "Any Greens" Pesto Pasta, 48, **49**

Asparagus
- Aunt Shelley's Fried Rice, 68, **69**
- Spring Minestrone, 132, **133**

Aunt Shelley's Fried Rice, 68, **69**

Avocado
- Avocado-Japapeño Green Goddess Dip, 176, **177**
- Corn, Zucchini and Tomato Salad, 30, **31**
- Green Gazpacho, 130, **131**

Avocado oil, 8

B
Baked Oatmeal, 196, **197**
Balsamic Brussels Sprouts and Butternut Squash, 158, **159**

Bananas
- Banana Snacking Cake, 198, **199**
- Chocolate, Almond and Banana Smoothie, 210, **211**

Basil, 29
- Browned Butter and Basil Trout, 80, **81**
- Cherry Tomato Confit with Elbow Pasta, 40, **41**
- Healthy Eggplant Parmesan with Pomodoro Sauce, 56, **57**, 58, **59**
- No-Boil Spinach Lasagna, 54, **55**
- Smoky Tomato-Bread Soup, 126, **127**
- Strawberry Bourbon Smash, 226
- Summer Farro "Risotto," 60, **61**

Beans. *See* Garbanzo beans; Green beans; Navy beans

Bean sprouts
- Ramen Made Right, 140, **141**

Beef
- Chile and Espresso–Rubbed Flank Steak, 118, **119**
- Grilled Tri-Tip with Black Bean Sauce, 116, **117**
- Harissa Beef Stew, 138, **139**
- Slow Cooker French Dip Sandwiches, 120, **121**

Beef stock
- Harissa Beef Stew, 138, **139**
- Slow Cooker French Dip Sandwiches, 120, **121**

Big-Batch Jalapeño Margaritas, 222, **223**

Black bean sauce
- Grilled Tri-Tip with Black Bean Sauce, 116, **117**

Blackberries
- Greek Yogurt and Berry Coffee Cake, 192, **193**
- Mixed Berry Crisp, 194, **195**
- Summer Sangria, 224, **225**

Black-eyed peas
- Instant Pot Black-Eyed Peas and Greens, 72, **73**

Blueberries
- Baked Oatmeal, 196, **197**
- Greek Yogurt and Berry Coffee Cake, 192, **193**
- Mixed Berry Crisp, 194, **195**
- Summer Sangria, 224, **225**

Bok choy
- Aunt Shelley's Fried Rice, 68, **69**
- Egg Roll in a Bowl, 66, **67**

Bone broth, 10

Bourbon, 216
- Strawberry Bourbon Smash, 226, **227**

Brandy, 224
- Winter Sangria, 224, **225**

Brazil nuts
- Chocolate, Almond and Banana Smoothie, 210, **211**

Breadcrumbs
- homemade, 52
- Pantry Pasta, 52, **53**

Bread-Free Romesco, 179, **181**

Broccoli
- Aunt Shelley's Fried Rice, 68, **69**

Broccolini
- Broccolini with Lemon Vinaigrette, 146, **147**
- steaming, 146

Broth
- bone, 10
- stock versus, 10

Brussels sprouts
- Balsamic Brussels Sprouts and Butternut Squash, 158, **159**
- Collard Greens and Brussels Sprout Salad, 26, **27**

Butter lettuce
- Butter Lettuce, Radish and Radicchio Salad, 24, **25**
- Ground Chicken in Lettuce Cups, 100, **101**
- Salmon Salad "Niçoise," 34, **35**

Buttermilk
- Avocado-Japapeño Green Goddess Dip, 176, **177**
- Banana Snacking Cake, 198, **199**
- Homemade Buttermilk Ranch Dressing, 38, **39**

Butternut squash
- Balsamic Brussels Sprouts and Butternut Squash, 158, **159**
- Seasonal Minestrone Variations, 134, **135**

C
Cabbage. *See* Green cabbage; Napa cabbage
- Seasonal Minestrone Variations, 134, **135**

Campari, 216
- Campari, OJ and Soda, 228, **229**
- Negroni Sbagliato, 228, **229**

Capers
- Halibut Poached in Lemon and White Wine, 82, **83**
- Red Snapper Roasted with Italian Salsa Verde, 86, **87**
- Spicy Rémoulade, **93**, 94

Carrots, 10
- Aunt Shelley's Fried Rice, 68, **69**
- Egg Roll in a Bowl, 66, **67**
- Ground Chicken in Lettuce Cups, 100, **101**
- Harissa Beef Stew, 138, **139**
- Healthy Eggplant Parmesan with Pomodoro Sauce, 56, **57**, 58, **59**
- Honey-Harissa Roasted Root Vegetables, 162, **163**
- Quick Lamb Ragu, 112, **113**
- Smoky Tomato-Bread Soup, 126, **127**
- Spicy Udon Noodles, 62, **63**
- Spring Minestrone, 132, **133**
- Vegetable Bolognese Rigatoni, 50, **51**

Casserole, Chicken Enchilada, 102, **103**
Cauliflower
    Bread-Free Romesco, 179, **181**
Celery
    Aunt Shelley's Fried Rice, 68, **69**
    Quick Lamb Ragu, 112, **113**
    Rotisserie Chicken and Wild Rice Soup, 136, **137**
    Salmon Salad "Niçoise," 34, **35**
    Smoky Tomato-Bread Soup, 126, **127**
    Spring Minestrone, 132, **133**
    Vegetable Bolognese Rigatoni, 50, **51**
Chana Masal, 70, **71**
Cheese, 12, 174. *See also* Cotija cheese; Feta cheese;
        Monterey Jack cheese; Mozzarella cheese;
        Parmigiano-Reggiano cheese; Pecorino cheese;
        Provolone cheese; Ricotta cheese
    boards for, 170
Chermoula, 92, **93**, 95
    Rosemary-Garlic Grilled Lamb Chops, 114, **115**
Cherries
    Baked Oatmeal, 196, **197**
Cherry tomatoes. *See also* Fire-roasted tomatoes; Tomatoes
    Cherry Tomato Confit with Elbow Pasta, 40, **41**
    Corn, Zucchini and Tomato Salad, 30, **31**
    Salmon Salad "Niçoise," 34, **35**
    Sockeye Salmon with Haricots Verts and Cherry
        Tomatoes, 88, **89**
    Summer Farro "Risotto," 60, **61**
Chia Seed Pudding, 208, **209**
Chicken
    Chicken Enchilada Casserole, 102, **103**
    Ground Chicken in Lettuce Cups, 100, **101**
    Rotisserie Chicken and Wild Rice Soup, 136, **137**
    Spatchcocked Chipotle-Lime Chicken, 104, **105**
Chicken stock
    Ground Chicken in Lettuce Cups, 100, **101**
    Harissa Beef Stew, 138, **139**
    Instant Pot Black-Eyed Peas and Greens, 72, **73**
    Mimi's Baked Potato Soup, 128, **129**
    Rotisserie Chicken and Wild Rice Soup, 136, **137**
    Smoky Tomato-Bread Soup, 126, **127**
    Spring Minestrone, 132, **133**
    Summer Farro "Risotto," 60, **61**
Chile powder, 118
    Chile and Espresso--Rubbed Flank Steak, 118, **119**
Chiles. *See* Chipotle chile; Green chile; Jalapeño chiles
Chipotle chile
    Spatchcocked Chipotle-Lime Chicken, 104, **105**
Chipotle-Lime Crema, **93**, 94
Chives
    Butter Lettuce, Radish and Radicchio Salad, 24, **25**
    Homemade Buttermilk Ranch Dressing, 38, **39**
    Red Cabbage Slaw, 32, **33**
Chocolate, Almond and Banana Smoothie, 210, **211**
Cilantro
    Avocado-Japapeño Green Goddess Dip, 176, **177**
    Chermoula, **93**, 95
    Corn, Zucchini and Tomato Salad, 30, **31**
Cocktail Nuts with Rosemary and Sage, 184, **185**
Cocktails, 213–230
    Aperol Margarita, **216**, 221
    Big-Batch Jalapeño Margaritas, 222, **223**
    Campari, OJ and Soda, 228, **229**
    Cocktails 101, 216, **217**
    Fresh Grapefruit Paloma, 218, **219**
    Ginger Margarita, **219**, 220
    Hot Honey Bees Knees, 226, **227**
    Negroni Sbagliato, 228, **229**
    Pineapple Rum Punch, 228, **227**
    Strawberry Bourbon Smash, 226, **227**

    Summer Sangria, 224, **225**
    Winter Sangria, 224, **225**
Coconut
    My Favorite Granola, 206, **207**
Coconut aminos
    Ground Chicken in Lettuce Cups, 100, **101**
Collard Greens and Brussels Sprout Salad, 26, **27**
Cooking oils, 8
Corn, Zucchini and Tomato Salad, 30, **31**
Cornichons
    Salmon Salad "Niçoise," 34, **35**
    Tartar Sauce, 93, 95
Cotija cheese
    Corn, Zucchini and Tomato Salad, 30, **31**
Cranberries
    Baked Oatmeal, 196, **197**
    Cranberry Streusel Muffins, 202, **203**
Creamy Hands-Off Polenta, 166, **167**
Crispy Smashed Potatoes, 160, **161**
Crudités board, veggies for, 172
D
Dates
    Chocolate, Almond and Banana Smoothie, 210, **211**
    Grandma's Date Squares, 200, **201**
Desserts, 189–210
    Baked Oatmeal, 196, **197**
    Banana Snacking Cake, 198, **199**
    Chia Seed Pudding, 208, **209**
    Cranberry Streusel Muffins, 202, **203**
    Grandma's Date Squares, 200, **201**
    Greek Yogurt and Berry Coffee Cake, 192, **193**
    Mixed Berry Crisp, 194, **195**
    My Favorite Granola, 206, **207**
    Popo's Melting Moments, 204, **205**
Dijon mustard
    Kale Caesar, 28, **29**
    Super Simple Salad Dressing, 40, **41**
Dill
    Deviled Eggs with Peas and Dill, 186, **187**
    Red Cabbage Slaw, 32, **33**
Dill pickles
    Salmon Salad "Niçoise," 34, **35**
    Tartar Sauce, **93**, 95
Dips
    Avocado-Japapeño Green Goddess Dip, 176, **177**
    White Bean Dip with Rosemary Olive Oil, 180, **181**
E
Edamame Hummus, **173**, **181**, 182
Egg noodles
    Peanut Noodles, 64, **65**
Eggplant
    Healthy Eggplant Parmesan with Pomodoro Sauce, 56, **57**, 58, **59**
    Summer Farro "Risotto," 60, **61**
Egg Roll in a Bowl, 66, **67**
Eggs
    Aunt Shelley's Fried Rice, 68, **69**
    Deviled Eggs with Peas and Dill, 186, **187**
    Greek Yogurt and Berry Coffee Cake, 192, **193**
    Ramen Made Right, 140, **141**
    Salmon Salad "Niçoise," 34, **35**
Enchilada sauce
    Chicken Enchilada Casserole, 102, **103**
Everything Bagel Seasoning, 152
F
Family dinner
    rules for, 18
    thoughts on, 16
Farro, Summer, "Risotto," 60, **61**
Feta cheese, 12

Corn, Zucchini and Tomato Salad, 30, **31**
dressing, 38
Simple Whipped Feta, 178
Fire-roasted tomatoes. *See also* Cherry tomatoes; Tomatoes
Smoky Tomato-Bread Soup, 126, **127**
Fish, 76–95
Blackened Redfish Tacos, 90, **91**
Browned Butter and Basil Trout, 80, **81**
Halibut Poached in Lemon and White Wine, 82, **83**
Panko-Crusted Fish Sticks, 78, **79**
Parchment Paper Fish Packets, 84, **85**
Red Snapper Roasted with Italian Salsa Verde, 86, **87**
Salmon Salad "Niçoise," 34, **35**
Sockeye Salmon with Haricots Verts and Cherry Tomatoes, 88, **89**
Fish sauces, 92, **93**
Chermoula, **93**, 95
Chipotle-Lime Crema, **93**, 94
Spicy Rémoulade, **93**, 94
Tartar Sauce, **93**, 95
Fresh Grapefruit Paloma, 218, **219**

G
Garbanzo beans
Chana Masala, 70, **71**
Spicy Roasted Garbanzos, 183
Garlic, 12
Chana Masala, 70, **71**
Cherry Tomato Confit with Elbow Pasta, 40, **41**
Corn, Zucchini and Tomato Salad, 30, **31**
Grilled Tri-Tip with Black Bean Sauce, 116, **117**
Honey-Hoisin Pork Tenderloin, 108, **109**
Kale Caesar, 28, **29**
Peanut Noodles, 64, **65**
Rosemary-Garlic Grilled Lamb Chop, 114, **115**
Summer Farro "Risotto," 60, **61**
Ginger beer, 216
Ginger Margarita, **219**, 220
Strawberry Bourbon Smash, 226, **227**
Grandma's Date Squares, 200, **201**
Grapefruit juice
Fresh Grapefruit Paloma, 218, **219**
Pineapple Rum Punch, 226, **227**
Grapes
Winter Sangria, 224, **225**
Greek yogurt
Avocado-Japapeño Green Goddess Dip, 176, **177**
Greek Yogurt and Berry Coffee Cake, 192, **193**
Homemade Buttermilk Ranch Dressing, 38, **39**
Simple Whipped Feta, 178
Green beans
Aunt Shelley's Fried Rice, 68, **69**
Salmon Salad "Niçoise," 34, **35**
Seasonal Minestrone Variations, 134, **135**
Sockeye Salmon with Haricots Verts and Cherry Tomatoes, 88, **89**
Za'atar Green Beans, 152, **153**
Green cabbage
Egg Roll in a Bowl, 66, **67**
Spicy Udon Noodles, 62, **63**
Green chile
Chana Masala, 70, **71**
Green Gazpacho, 130, **131**
Green onions
Aunt Shelley's Fried Rice, 68, **69**
Avocado-Japapeño Green Goddess Dip, 176, **177**
Butter Lettuce, Radish and Radicchio Salad, 24, **25**
Corn, Zucchini and Tomato Salad, 30, **31**
Ground Chicken in Lettuce Cups, 100, **101**
Honey-Hoisin Pork Tenderloin, 108, **109**
Spicy Udon Noodles, 62, **63**

H
Harissa paste
Harissa Beef Stew, 138, **139**
Honey-Harissa Roasted Root Vegetables, 162, **163**
Healthy Eggplant Parmesan with Pomodoro Sauce, 56, **57**, 58, **59**
Herbs. *See also specific*
fresh versus dried, 12
Hoagie rolls
Slow Cooker French Dip Sandwiches, 120, **121**
Hoisin sauce
Peanut Noodles, 64, **65**
Homemade Za'atar, 152
Honey-Harissa Roasted Root Vegetables, 162, **163**
Hot Honey Bees Knees, 226, **227**

I
Ingredients, importance of good, 8, 10, 12
Instant Pot
Creamy Hands-Off Polenta, 166, **167**
Dry-Rubbed Pulled Pork, 106, **107**
Harissa Beef Stew, 138, **139**
Instant Pot Black-Eyed Peas and Greens, 72, **73**
Rotisserie Chicken and Wild Rice Soup, 136, **137**
Smoky Tomato-Bread Soup, 126, **127**

J
Jalapeño chiles
Avocado-Japapeño Green Goddess Dip, 176, **177**
Big-Batch Jalapeño Margaritas, 222, **223**
Corn, Zucchini and Tomato Salad, 30, **31**
Homemade Buttermilk Ranch Dressing, 38
Spatchcocked Chipotle-Lime Chicken, 104, **105**
Juices. *See also* Grapefruit juice; Lemon juice; Lime juice; Orange juice
fresh squeezed, 10

K
Kale
"Any Greens" Pesto Pasta, 48, **49**
Kale Caesar, 28, **29**
Seasonal Minestrone Variations, 134, **135**
Kitchen equipment, 230–231

L
Lamb
Quick Lamb Ragu, 112, **113**
Rosemary-Garlic Grilled Lamb Chop, 114, **115**
Leafy greens
"Any Greens" Pesto Pasta, 48, **49**
Ramen Made Right, 140, **141**
Spring Minestrone, 132, **133**
Leeks
cleaning, 50
Instant Pot Black-Eyed Peas and Greens, 72, **73**
Mimi's Baked Potato Soup, 128, **129**
Rotisserie Chicken and Wild Rice Soup, 136, **137**
Spring Minestrone, 132, **133**
Vegetable Bolognese Rigatoni, 50, **51**
Lemon juice, 10
Kale Caesar, 28, **29**
Rosemary-Garlic Grilled Lamb Chops, 114, **115**
Lemon vinaigrette, 146
Lettuce. *See* Butter lettuce
Lime juice, 10
Aperol Margarita, **217**, **219**, 221
Ginger Margarita, **219**, 220
Spatchcocked Chipotle-Lime Chicken, 104, **105**

M
Mains. *See* Fish; Meatless Mains; Meaty Mains
Meatless Mains, 43–72
"Any Greens" Pesto Pasta, 48, **49**
Aunt Shelley's Fried Rice, 68, **69**
Chana Masala, 70, **71**

Cherry Tomato Confit with Elbow Pasta, 40, 41
Egg Roll in a Bowl, 66, **67**
Healthy Eggplant Parmesan with Pomodoro Sauce, 56, **57**, **58**, **59**
Instant Pot Black-Eyed Peas and Greens, 72, **73**
No-Boil Spinach Lasagna, 54, **55**
Pantry Pasta, 52, **53**
Peanut Noodles, 64, **65**
Spicy Udon Noodles, 62, **63**
Summer Farro "Risotto," 60, **61**
Vegetable Bolognese Rigatoni, 50, **51**
Meaty Mains, 97–120
Chicken Enchilada Casserole, 102, **103**
Chile and Espresso--Rubbed Flank Steak, 118, **119**
Dry-Rubbed Pulled Pork, 106, **107**
Grilled Tri-Tip with Black Bean Sauce, 116, **117**
Ground Chicken in Lettuce Cups, 100, **101**
Honey-Hoisin Pork Tenderloin, 108, **109**
Quick Lamb Ragu, 112, **113**
Rosemary-Garlic Grilled Lamb Chops, 114, **115**
Slow Cooker Carnitas Tacos, 110, **111**
Slow Cooker French Dip Sandwiches, 120, **121**
Spatchcocked Chipotle-Lime Chicken, 104, **105**
Mimi's Baked Potato Soup, 128, **129**
Minestrone
seasonal variations of, 134, **135**
spring, 132, **133**
Mint
Butter Lettuce, Radish and Radicchio Salad, 24, **25**
Homemade Buttermilk Ranch Dressing, 38, **39**
Mint jelly, 114
Mise en place, 14
Mixed Berry Crisp, 194, **195**
Monterey Jack cheese
Chicken Enchilada Casserole, 102, **103**
Mozzarella cheese
Healthy Eggplant Parmesan with Pomodoro Sauce, 56, **57**, **58**, **59**
No-Boil Spinach Lasagna, 54, **55**
Mushrooms
Egg Roll in a Bowl, 66, **67**
Ground Chicken in Lettuce Cups, 100, **101**
Ramen Made Right, 140, **141**
Rotisserie Chicken and Wild Rice Soup, 136, **137**
Vegetable Bolognese Rigatoni, 50, **51**
Mustard. *See* Dijon mustard
My Favorite Granola, 206, **207**

N
Napa cabbage
Egg Roll in a Bowl, 66, **67**
Spicy Udon Noodles, 62, **63**
Navy beans
Spring Minestrone, 132, **133**
White Bean Dip with Rosemary Olive Oil, 180, **181**
Nectarines
Summer Sangria, 224
Negroni Sbagliato, 228, **229**
No-Boil Spinach Lasagna, 54, **55**
Nori sheet
Ramen Made Right, 140, **141**
Nuts. *See* Almonds; Brazil nuts; Pecans; Pine nuts; Pistachios; Walnuts
Cocktail Nuts with Rosemary and Sage, 184, **185**

O
Oats
Baked Oatmeal, 196, **197**
Grandma's Date Squares, 200, **201**
My Favorite Granola, 206, **207**
Olive oil, 8
Onions. *See also* Green onions; Red onions
Aunt Shelley's Fried Rice, 68, **69**
Chana Masala, 70, **71**
Egg Roll in a Bowl, 66, **67**
Harissa Beef Stew, 138, **139**
Mimi's Baked Potato Soup, 128, **129**
Rotisserie Chicken and Wild Rice Soup, 136, **137**
Slow Cooker Carnitas Tacos, 110, **111**
Smoky Tomato-Bread Soup, 126, **127**
Summer Farro "Risotto," 60, **61**
Vegetable Bolognese Rigatoni, 50, **51**
Orange juice, 10
Aperol Margarita, **217**, **219**, 221
Campari, OJ and Soda, 228, **229**
Spatchcocked Chipotle-Lime Chicken, 104, **105**
Oregano, 9, 29
Cherry Tomato Confit with Elbow Pasta, 46, **47**
Organics, 10
Oven-Roasted Mini Sweet Peppers, 150, **151**

P
Pan-Roasted Shishito Peppers, 148, **149**
Parchment paper, 76
Parchment Paper Fish Packets, 84, **85**
Popo's Melting Moments, 204, **205**
Parmigiano-Reggiano cheese, 12
"Any Greens" Pesto Pasta, 48, **49**
Collard Greens and Brussels Sprout Salad, 26, **27**
Healthy Eggplant Parmesan with Pomodoro Sauce, 56, **57**, **58**, **59**
Kale Caesar, 28, **29**
No-Boil Spinach Lasagna, 54, **55**
Pantry Pasta, 52, **53**
Quick Lamb Ragu, 112, **113**
Spring Minestrone, 132, **133**
Summer Farro "Risotto," 60, **61**
Vegetable Bolognese Rigatoni, 50, **51**
Parsley
"Any Greens" Pesto Pasta, 48, **49**
Avocado-Japapeño Green Goddess Dip, 176, **177**
Chermoula, **93**, 95
Homemade Buttermilk Ranch Dressing, 38, **39**
Red Cabbage Slaw, 32, **33**
Parsnips
Honey-Harissa Roasted Root Vegetables, 162, **163**
Pasta
"Any Greens" Pesto Pasta, 48, **49**
Cherry Tomato Confit with Elbow Pasta, 40, **41**
No-Boil Spinach Lasagna, 54, **55**
Pantry Pasta, 52, **53**
Peanut Noodles, 64, **65**
Vegetable Bolognese Rigatoni, 50, **51**
Peaches
Summer Sangria, 224, **225**
Peanut Noodles, 64, **65**
Pears
Winter Sangria, 224, **225**
Peas. *See also* Black-eyed peas; Sugar snap peas
Deviled Eggs with Peas and Dill, 186, **187**
Spring Minestrone, 132, **133**
Pecans
"Any Greens" Pesto Pasta, 48, **49**
Collard Greens and Brussels Sprout Salad, 26, **27**
Mixed Berry Crisp, 194, **195**
My Favorite Granola, 206, **207**
Pecorino cheese
Collard Greens and Brussels Sprout Salad, 26, **27**
Pellegrino, 216
Peppers, 8. *See also* Red bell peppers; Shishito peppers
Oven-Roasted Mini Sweet Peppers, 150, **151**
Persian cucumbers, 130
Green Gazpacho, 130, **131**

Pickles. *See* Dill pickles
Pimentón de la Vera, 126
    Smoky Tomato-Bread Soup, 126, **127**
Pineapple Rum Punch, 226, **227**
Pine nuts
    "Any Greens" Pesto Pasta, 48, **49**
Pinto beans
    Chicken Enchilada Casserole, 102, **103**
Pistachios
    "Any Greens" Pesto Pasta, 48, **49**
Polenta, Creamy Hands-Off, 166, **167**
Pollan, Michael, 8
Pomegranate juice
    Winter Sangria, 224
Pomegranate seeds
    Collard Greens and Brussels Sprout Salad, 26, **27**
    Winter Sangria, 224
Pomodoro Sauce
    Healthy Eggplant Parmesan with Pomodoro Sauce, 56, **57**, 58, **59**
    No-Boil Spinach Lasagna, 54, **55**
Popo's Melting Moments, 204, **205**
Pork
    Dry-Rubbed Pulled Pork, 32, 106, **107**
    Honey-Hoisin Pork Tenderloin, 108, **109**
    Slow Cooker Carnitas Tacos, 110, **111**
Potatoes
    Crispy Smashed Potatoes, 160, **161**
    Harissa Beef Stew, 138, **139**
    Mimi's Baked Potato Soup, 128, **129**
    Salmon Salad "Niçoise," 34, **35**
    Seasonal Minestrone Variations, 134, **135**
Prosecco
    Negroni Sbagliato, 228, **229**
    Sorbet-Prosecco Spritz, 230, **231**
    Summer Sangria, 224, **225**
Provolone cheese
    Slow Cooker French Dip Sandwiches, 120, **121**
Pumpkin seeds
    Green Gazpacho, 130
    My Favorite Granola, 206, **207**

Q
Quick-Pickled Red Onions, 36, **37**
    Kale Caesar, 28, **29**
    Salmon Salad "Niçoise," 34, **35**

R
Radicchio, Butter Lettuce, Radish and Salad, 24, **25**
Radishes, Butter Lettuce, and Radicchio Salad, 24, **25**
Raisins
    Baked Oatmeal, 196, **197**
Ramen Made Right, 140, **141**
Raspberries
    Greek Yogurt and Berry Coffee Cake, 192, **193**
    Mixed Berry Crisp, 194, **195**
Recipe, timing of, 14
Red bell peppers
    Bread-Free Romesco, 179
    Spicy Udon Noodles, 62, **63**
Red Cabbage Slaw, 32, **33**
Red onion
    Balsamic Brussels Sprouts and Butternut Squash, 158, **159**
    Quick-Pickled Red Onions, 36, **37**
Red wine
    Vegetable Bolognese Rigatoni, 50, **51**
Red wine vinegar
    Red Cabbage Slaw, 32, **33**
    Red Snapper Roasted with Italian Salsa Verde, 86, **87**
Rice
    Aunt Shelley's Fried Rice, 68, **69**
    Chana Masala, 70, **71**
    Honey-Hoisin Pork Tenderloin, 108, **109**
    Rotisserie Chicken and Wild Rice Soup, 136, **137**
Rice vinegar
    Quick-Pickled Red Onions, 36, **37**
    Rice Vinegar-Soy Sauce, 100
Ricotta cheese
    No-Boil Spinach Lasagna, 54, **55**
Rigatoni, Vegetable Bolognese, 50, **51**
Roasted Zucchini with Marcona Almond—Rosemary Crunch, 156, **157**
Rosemary
    Cocktail Nuts with Rosemary and Sage, 184, **185**
    Roasted Zucchini with Marcona Almond—Rosemary Crunch, 156, **157**
    Rosemary-Garlic Grilled Lamb Chop, 114, **115**
    White Bean Dip with Rosemary Olive Oil, 180, **181**
Rotisserie Chicken and Wild Rice Soup, 136, **137**
Rum, Pineapple, Punch, 226, **227**
Rutabaga
    Honey-Harissa Roasted Root Vegetables, 162, **163**

S
Sage, Cocktail Nuts with Rosemary and, 184, **185**
Salad dressings
    Homemade Buttermilk Ranch Dressing, 38, **39**
    Super Simple Salad Dressing, 40, **41**
Salads, 22–41
    Butter Lettuce, Radish and Radicchio Salad, 24, **25**
    Collard Greens and Brussels Sprout Salad, 26, **27**
    Corn, Zucchini and Tomato Salad, 30, **31**
    Kale Caesar, 28, **29**
    Quick-Pickled Red Onions, 36, **37**
    Salmon Salad "Niçoise," 34, **35**
Salmon
    Salmon Salad "Niçoise," 34, **35**
    Sockeye Salmon with Haricots Verts and Cherry Tomatoes, 88, **89**
Salt, 8
Sandwiches
    Dry-Rubbed Pulled Pork, 106, **107**
    Slow Cooker French Dip Sandwiches, 120, **121**
Seeds. *See* Pomegrante seeds; Pumpkin seeds
Shallots
    Healthy Eggplant Parmesan with Pomodoro Sauce, 56, **57**, 58, **59**
    Spatchcocked Chipotle-Lime Chicken, 104, **105**
    Super Simple Salad Dressing, 40, **41**
Shishito peppers, Pan-Roasted, 148, **149**
Shopping list, writing a, 14
Sides, 143–166
    Balsamic Brussels Sprouts and Butternut Squash, 158, **159**
    Broccolini with Lemon Vinaigrette, 146, **147**
    Creamy Hands-Off Polenta, 166, **167**
    Crispy Smashed Potatoes, 160, **161**
    Honey-Harissa Roasted Root Vegetables, 162, **163**
    Oven-Roasted Mini Sweet Peppers, 150, **151**
    Pan-Roasted Shishito Peppers, 148, **149**
    Roasted Zucchini with Marcona Almond—Rosemary Crunch, 156, **157**
    Soy-Sesame Spinach, 154, **155**
    Sweet Potatoes with Brown Sugar Glaze, 164, **165**
    Za'atar Green Beans, 152, **153**
Simple Whipped Feta, 171, 178, **181**
Slaw, Red Cabbage, 32, **33**
Slow cooker
    Dry-Rubbed Pulled Pork, 106, **107**
    Slow Cooker Carnitas Tacos, 110, **111**
    Slow Cooker French Dip Sandwiches, 120, **121**
Smart, Marcia, 6, **7**
Smartinthekitchen.com, 14
Smart Knife Skills, 14

Smoky Tomato-Bread Soup, 126, **127**
Smoothie, Chocolate, Almond and Banana, 210, **211**
Snacks, 169–186
    Avocado–Jalapeño Green Goddess Dip, 176, **177**
    Board Checklist for, 172, **173**, 174, **175**
    Bread-Free Romesco, 179, **181**
    Cocktail Nuts with Rosemary and Sage, 184, **185**
    Edamame Hummus, **173**, **181**, 182
    Simple Whipped Feta, 171, 178, **181**
    Snack Board Checklist, 172, **173**, 174, **175**
    Spicy Roasted Garbanzos, 183
    White Bean Dip with Rosemary Olive Oil, 180, **181**
Souper Cubes, 124
Soups
    Green Gazpacho, 130, **131**
    Mimi's Baked Potato Soup, 128, **129**
    Ramen Made Right, 140, **141**
    Rotisserie Chicken and Wild Rice Soup, 136, **137**
    Seasonal Minestrone Variations, 134, **135**
    Smoky Tomato-Bread Soup, 126, **127**
    Spring Minestrone, 132, **133**
Soy beans, 10
Soy sauce, 10
    Aunt Shelley's Fried Rice, 68, **69**
    Egg Roll in a Bowl, 66, **67**
    Ground Chicken in Lettuce Cups, 100, **101**
    Honey-Hoisin Pork Tenderloin, 108, **109**
    Rice Vinegar-Soy Sauce, 100
    Soy-Sesame Spinach, 154, **155**
    Spicy Udon Noodles, 62, **63**
Soy-Sesame Spinach, 154, **155**
Spices. *See also specific by name*
    organizing, 12
Spicy Rémoulade, **93**, 94
    Panko-Crusted Fish Sticks, 78, **79**
Spicy Roasted Garbanzos, 183
    Kale Caesar, 28, **29**
Spicy Udon Noodles, 62, **63**
Spinach
    "Any Greens" Pesto Pasta, 48, **49**
    Instant Pot Black-Eyed Peas and Greens, 72, **73**
    No-Boil Spinach Lasagna, 54, **55**
    Seasonal Minestrone Variations, 134, **135**
    Soy-Sesame Spinach, 154, **155**
Spring Minestrone, 132, **133**
Squash. *See* Butternut squash
Stew, Harissa Beef, 138, **139**
Stock. *See also* Beef stock; Broth; Chicken stock; Vegetable stock
    versus broth, 10
Strawberry Bourbon Smash, 226, **227**
Substitutions, 14
Sugar snap peas
    Aunt Shelley's Fried Rice, 68, **69**
    Spring Minestrone, 132, **133**
Summer Farro "Risotto," 60, **61**
Summer Sangria, 224, **225**
Sunflower seeds
    Green Gazpacho, 130, **131**
Super Simple Salad Dressing, 22
    Butter Lettuce, Radish and Radicchio Salad, 24, **25**
    Collard Greens and Brussels Sprout Salad, 26, **27**
    Salmon Salad "Niçoise," 34, **35**
Sweet potatoes
    Honey-Harissa Roasted Root Vegetables, 162, **163**
    Seasonal Minestrone Variations, 134, **135**
    Sweet Potatoes with Brown Sugar Glaze, 164, **165**
Swiss chard
    "Any Greens" Pesto Pasta, 48, **49**
    Instant Pot Black-Eyed Peas and Greens, 72, **73**

    Seasonal Minestrone Variations, 134, **135**
T
Tacos, Slow Cooker Carnitas, 110, **111**
Tahini
    Edamame Hummus, **173**, **181**, 182
Tamari, 10
    Ground Chicken in Lettuce Cups, 100, **101**
Tangerines
    Winter Sangria, 224, **225**
Tartar Sauce, 92, **93**, 95
Tasting as you go, 14
Tequila
    Aperol Margarita, **216**, 221
    Big-Batch Jalapeño Margaritas, 222, **223**
    Ginger Margarita, **219**, 220
Thyme
    Cherry Tomato Confit with Elbow Pasta, 40, **41**
    Oven-Roasted Mini Sweet Peppers, 150, **151**
    Quick Lamb Ragu, 112, **113**
    Rotisserie Chicken and Wild Rice Soup, 136, **137**
Tofu
    Ramen Made Right, 140, **141**
Tomatoes. *See* Cherry tomatoes; Fire-roasted tomatoes
    Chana Masala, 70, **71**
    Green Gazpacho, 130, **131**
    Healthy Eggplant Parmesan with Pomodoro Sauce, 56, **57**, 58, **59**
    Peanut Noodles, 64, **65**
    Quick Lamb Ragu, 112, **113**
    Seasonal Minestrone Variations, 134, **135**
    Vegetable Bolognese Rigatoni, 50, **51**
Tomato sauce
    Chicken Enchilada Casserole, 102, **103**
    No-Boil Spinach Lasagna, 54, **55**
Topo Chico, 216
Tortillas
    Chicken Enchilada Casserole, 102, **103**
U
Udon noodles, Spicy, 62, **63**
V
Vegetable Bolognese Rigatoni, 50, **51**
Vegetable stock
    Summer Farro "Risotto," 60, **61**
Vermouth, 216
Vinegar. *See* Apple cider vinegar; Red wine vinegar; Rice vinegar; White wine vinegar
W
Walnuts
    "Any Greens" Pesto Pasta, 48, **49**
Whiskey, 216
    Strawberry Bourbon Smash, 226, **227**
White Bean Dip with Rosemary Olive Oil, 180, **181**
White wine
    Halibut Poached in Lemon and White Wine, 82, **83**
White wine vinegar
    Quick-Pickled Red Onions, 36, **37**
Wine. *See* Red wine; White wine
Winter Sangria, 224, **225**
Z
Za'atar Green Beans, 152, **153**
Zest, 10
Zucchini
    Corn, Zucchini and Tomato Salad, 30, **31**
    Roasted Zucchini with Marcona Almond–Rosemary Crunch, 156, **157**
    Seasonal Minestrone Variations, 134, **135**
    Summer Farro "Risotto," 60, **61**

> Her mission is to help home cooks enjoy more family meals.

About the Author

A graduate of the professional culinary program at Tante Marie Cooking School in San Francisco, Marcia Smart is a cooking instructor, recipe developer and food writer, and creator of *Smart in the Kitchen* and *Smart in the Kitchen School*. Through *Smart in the Kitchen*, Marcia hosts cooking classes, culinary team-building events and cooking retreats. She blogs about meal planning, easy weeknight recipes and healthy family dinners at **smartinthekitchen.com** and runs an online cooking school at **smartinthekitchenschool.com**. Her mission is to help home cooks enjoy more family meals.

Marcia began her career in the editorial department at *Parenting* magazine and worked as a producer for *Women.com*, a food editor for *7x7* magazine in San Francisco, and a contributing editor and restaurant critic at *Houston Modern Luxury* magazine. Her freelance articles and recipes have appeared in *Cooking Light*, *Parenting, Houston Chronicle, Sunset, Robb Report*, *Houston Modern Luxury*, *Houston CityBook*, *Parenting Travel*, *BabyTalk*, *BabyCenter.com* and *Safeway* magazine. Marcia was selected multiple years as a contributor for *Cooking Light's Annual Recipes* cookbooks. You can catch Marcia as a regular cooking guest on *HoustonLife*, an NBC lifestyle show. She has also appeared on *Hallmark Home & Family* and *Great Day Houston*.

You can visit Marcia at **smartinthekitchen.com**, **smartinthekitchenschool.com** and on Instagram **@smartinthekitchen**.

Apple Custard

APPLE custard is decidedly new. To make it, beat three eggs in a quart-sized custard dish. Stir in one cupful of sugar and the grated rind of a large orange. Add three cupfuls of milk and two cupfuls of sliced apple. Mix well and set in a dish of hot water in a hot oven. Cook until the custard is firm, and serve with or without whipped cream or prepared marshmallow or a meringue of egg whites.

Apple Custard Pie

THE same mixture may be used in half the quantity for the making of an apple custard pie. In this case the pie-plate is merely lined with pastry, the mixture poured in, and the pie set in a hot oven for the first ten minutes, when the heat should be reduced for the remainder of the baking-time.

Strawberry Pie or ta[rt]

Glaze

1 cup sugar
3 tablespoon cornstarch
1 teaspoon lemon juice
1 cup liquid, consisting [of]
berries crushed and
water to fill a cup.
Cook until thick, wh[en]
pour over berries in [pie]
[shell] and top with whip[ped cream]
Takes 2 boxes ber[ries]

Single crust.
Use ¼ oil 2 tbs. erased 2 drops coloring
1 cup + 2 tbs flour ½ salt 2 tbs
water. Flute prick dough on
bottom + sides. Bake 425° for
12-15 minutes until Brown
as desired.

Lemon Pie
Pie Crust of oil
2 cups flour
1 tsp salt
1 tbsp sugar
1 c. oil
6 tbsp water fork in bowl
Stir with fork into pa[ste]
Roll between wax pap[er]
475° 8-10 B[rown]

Lemon P[ie]
[1 c]an Eaglebrand m[ilk]
[? c] lemon juice
[1 l]arge cool whip
[Mix] altogether, po[ur into]
[gra]ham cracker cr[ust]